CHRISTMAS

There is nothing that I can give you which you have not,
but there is much that, while I cannot give, you can take.

No heaven can come to us
unless our hearts find rest in it today.

Take Heaven.

No peace lies in the future
which is not hidden in this present instant.

Take Peace.

The gloom of the world is but a shadow.
Behind it, yet within our reach, is joy.

Take Joy!

And so, at this Christmas time,
I greet you with the prayer that for you, now and forever,
the day breaks and the shadows flee away.

FRA GIOVANNI
1513

CHRISTMAS

An Annual Treasury

VOLUME SIXTY-SIX

Augsburg

MINNEAPOLIS

The Christmas Crèche

WHEN I WAS GROWING UP, it never really felt like Christmas until we'd assembled our nativity set under the tree. This was no priceless heirloom crèche: my brother and I had chosen the figures one year from counters at our local Woolworth's. Dad built a wonderful little stable from scrap wood and drilled a hole in its back wall for a Christmas bulb. Mom selected her finest hand-sewn linen napkin to lay beneath the figures. Once we'd arranged the characters in their proper places, we gathered around to hear Dad read the story from Luke's Gospel. As we stared into the soft glow of our crèche and listened to those timeless words, we knew that Christmas had truly arrived.

The crèche became a regular part of our celebrations. It drew us together as a family, and it pointed us to the message and promise of Christmas.

This year's Annual is filled with features that can draw you and your loved ones together around the meaning of Christmas.

- Enlist friends and family to help you create a nativity set you'll be proud to display. Set aside a wintry Saturday, make plenty of cookies and hot chocolate, then follow the simple instructions in *Crafting a Christmas Crèche* (p. 38).

- During the days before and after Christmas, use your crèche as a setting for family devotions. *Gather Around the Manger* (p. 16) is a collection of readings, carols, prayers, and activities built around the assembling of a nativity set.

- Holidays are wonderful times to read together. Two ideal selections for reading aloud are the beautiful *Christmas Story* from the Gospels of St. Luke and St. Matthew (p. 6), and *A Christmas for Greccio* (p. 22), a delightful children's tale about St. Francis and the first crèche.

- Take a tour of the Bavarian National Museum's world-famous crèche collection in *The Nativity in Miniature* (p. 26). As you study the history of the crèche and view the marvelous collection, you'll discover ways to enrich the traditions surrounding your own nativity set.

- Invite relatives from near and far—or create a "Christmas family" of friends and neighbors—to help you sample the festive food and activities described in *Merry Memories: A Christmas Brunch* (p. 60).

It's been a long time since those childhood Christmases around the crèche. My father died some years ago. My brother is the pastor of a church hundreds of miles from the town where we grew up. Christmas is one of his busiest times, so he and his family have to stay close to home. But most years I still make the trip to spend the holiday with my mom.

On Christmas Eve, after we've been to church and made our visits to relatives, we sit by Mom's small tree and open our gifts. Then, in the light of that old nativity set, I read the Christmas Gospel from St. Luke. As we sit in the glow of the crèche and hear again that timeless story, our family seems complete once more. And it feels like Christmas.

Wishing you a warm, *family* Christmas filled with the message and promise of God's love!

Bob Klausmeier

EDITOR

Editor: Robert Klausmeier; Art direction and design: Ellen Maly, Marti Naughton, and Craig Claeys; Production editor: Elizabeth Boyce. Cover photography: Leo Kim. Half-title illustration: Dan Reed. Initial letter illustration: Brian Jensen. With thanks to Pam McClanahan and Ann Potthoff for their assistance.

Acknowledgments: Scripture text for "The Christmas Story" is taken from *The Holy Bible, New King James Version*, copyright © 1979, 1980, 1982 Thomas Nelson, Inc. Used by permission. All other scripture quotations are from the New Revised Standard Version Bible, copyright © 1989 by the Division of Christian Education of the National Council of the Churches of Christ in the USA and used by permission. Text, tunes, and settings of "Infant Holy, Infant Lowly," "Silent Night," "Joy to the World," and "Let Our Gladness Have No End" are taken from *Lutheran Book of Worship*, copyright © 1978. Used by permission. "Christmas Stollen" text copyright © Bette Anne Gibson-Rieth. Used by permission. "Gather Around the Manger" text copyright © Debbie Trafton O'Neal. Used by permission. "A Christmas for Greccio" text copyright © Bob Hartman. Used by permission. "The Nativity in Miniature" text copyright © Nan Bauroth. Used by permission. "That Christmas Feeling" text copyright © Lynea Bowdish. Used by permission. "Crafting a Christmas Crèche" text copyright © Charlene Hiebert. Used by permission. "The Birthplace of God" text copyright © Phillip Gugel. Used by permission. "No Room for Jesus in Jonesboro" text copyright © Elizabeth Rice Handford. Used by permission.

Contents

The Christmas Story

ACCORDING TO ST. LUKE AND ST. MATTHEW

THE ANGEL GABRIEL was sent by God to a city of Galilee named Nazareth, to a virgin betrothed to a man whose name was Joseph, of the house of David. The virgin's name was Mary.

And having come in, the angel said to her, "Rejoice, highly favored one, the Lord is with you; blessed are you among women!"

But when she saw him, she was troubled at his saying, and considered what manner of greeting this was.

Then the angel said to her, "Do not be afraid, Mary, for you have found favor with God. And behold, you will conceive in your womb and bring forth a Son, and shall call His name Jesus. He will be great, and will be called the Son of the Highest; and the Lord God will give Him the throne of His father David. And He will reign over the house of Jacob forever, and of His kingdom there will be no end."

Then Mary said to the angel, "How can this be, since I do not know a man?"

And the angel answered and said to her, "The Holy Spirit will come upon you, and the power of the Highest will overshadow you; therefore, also, that Holy One who is to be born will be called the Son of God.

"Now indeed, Elizabeth your relative has also conceived a son in her old age; and this is now the sixth month for her who was called barren. For with God nothing will be impossible."

Then Mary said, "Behold the maidservant of the Lord! Let it be to me according to your word." And the angel departed from her.

And it came to pass in those days that a decree went out from Caesar Augustus that all the world should be registered. This census first took place while Quirinius was governing Syria. So all went to be registered, everyone to his own city.

Joseph also went up from Galilee, out of the city of Nazareth, into Judea, to the city of David, which is called Bethlehem, because he was of the house and lineage of David, to be registered with Mary, his betrothed wife, who was with child.

So it was, that while they were there, the days were completed for her to be delivered.

And she brought forth her firstborn Son, and wrapped Him in swaddling cloths, and laid Him in a manger, because there was no room for them in the inn.

Now there were in the same country shepherds living out in the fields, keeping watch over their flock by night. And behold, an angel of the Lord stood before them, and the glory of the Lord shone around them, and they were greatly afraid.

Then the angel said to them, "Do not be afraid, for behold, I bring you good tidings of great joy which will be to all people. For there is born to you this day in the city of David a Savior, who is Christ the Lord. And this will be the sign to you: You will find a Babe wrapped in swaddling cloths, lying in a manger."

And suddenly there was with the angel a multitude of the heavenly host praising God and saying:

"Glory to God in the highest, and on earth peace, goodwill toward men!"

So it was, when the angels had gone away from them into heaven, that the shepherds said to one another, "Let us now go to Bethlehem and see this thing that has come to pass, which the Lord has made known to us."

And they came with haste and found Mary and Joseph, and the Babe lying in a manger. Now when they had seen Him, they made widely known the saying which was told them concerning this Child. And all those who heard it marveled at those things which were told them by the shepherds. But Mary kept all these things and pondered them in her heart. Then the shepherds returned, glorifying and praising God for all the things that they had heard and seen, as it was told them.

Now after Jesus was born in Bethlehem of Judea in the days of Herod the king, behold, wise men from the East came to Jerusalem, saying, "Where is He who has been born King of the Jews? For we have seen His star in the East and have come to worship Him."

When Herod the king heard this, he was troubled, and all Jerusalem with him. And when he had gathered all the chief priests and scribes of the people together, he inquired of them where the Christ was to be born.

So they said to him, "In Bethlehem of Judea, for thus it is written by the prophet: 'But you, Bethlehem, in the land of Judah, are not the least among the rulers of Judah; for out of you shall come a Ruler who will shepherd My people Israel.'"

Then Herod, when he had secretly called the wise men, determined from them what time the star appeared. And he sent them to Bethlehem and said, "Go and search carefully for the young Child, and when you have found Him, bring back word to me, that I may come and worship Him also."

When they heard the king, they departed; and behold, the star which they had seen in the East went before them, till it came and stood over where the young Child was. When they saw the star, they rejoiced with exceedingly great joy.

And when they had come into the house, they saw the young Child with Mary His mother, and fell down and worshiped Him. And when they had opened their treasures, they presented gifts to Him: gold, frankincense, and myrrh.

Then, being divinely warned in a dream that they should not return to Herod, they departed for their own country another way.

Now when they had departed, behold, an angel of the Lord appeared to Joseph in a dream, saying, "Arise, take the young Child and His mother, flee to Egypt, and stay there until I bring you word; for Herod will seek the young Child to destroy Him."

When he arose, he took the young Child and His mother by night and departed for Egypt, and was there until the death of Herod, that it might be fulfilled which was spoken by the Lord through the prophet, saying, "Out of Egypt I called My Son."

Now when Herod was dead, behold, an angel of the Lord appeared in a dream to Joseph in Egypt, saying, "Arise, take the young Child and His mother, and go to the land of Israel, for those who sought the young Child's life are dead."

Then he arose, took the young Child and His mother, and came into the land of Israel. ❧

Randy Beumer is a free-lance artist devoted to illustrating biblical text and teachings. He lives and works in Salt Lake City, Utah.

The Christmas Story

*Her frantic search to find "something special" for Christmas brunch
leads Gladys Ernestine on a journey into the past,
where she encounters a donkey named Leopold, a live nativity,
and a mysterious, wonderful experience of Christmas love.*

Christmas Stollen

BETTE ANNE GIBSON-RIETH

THE INSTANT THE BUS PULLED away, Gladys Ernestine wished she were still on it. Dusk had settled on the city. Icy snow fell. She had not noticed the snow and darkness through the smudgy windows of the bus. Her mind had been busy with memories. Only after the bus doors slapped shut behind her did she realize how the weather had changed. The sidewalk before her glistened with winter's treachery. How on earth had she ended up here?

"Stollen," she said aloud.

A good thing Helen isn't here, she thought. "Gladys," her sister would say, "I swear you're going dotty on me."

Helen had called last night to remind Gladys that Christmas brunch would begin at eleven. "Not cranberry nut bread again," Helen had said when Gladys told her what she was bringing to the family celebration.

"It's a tradition," Gladys said.

"It's dry. And anyway, Raymond and his family are coming."

Raymond was Helen's newest friend. Gladys hesitated to refer to him as her sister's boyfriend. At their age, she thought it a frivolous thing to call a man.

"Don't be such a stick-in-the-mud, Gladys. You've brought that same bread for years. Bring something different this year. Something special."

"We'll see who's a stick-in-the-mud. We'll see who's dotty," Gladys had said after she hung up the phone.

First thing this morning when she'd arrived at work, Gladys had tried to think of something special to bring to the brunch. Something that would please Helen. While she thought, she patted her gray curls, straightened her name tag, the one that read CONWAY'S—THE CUSTOMER IS OUR FIRST CONCERN, and put on her best holiday smile—only a second before Mr. Barth made his morning rounds through the department.

"Good morning, Gladys," he said, tapping the men's accessory counter with his fingertips. "Ready to sell some ties?"

"Oh, yes," she said brightly, although she was tired of selling ties. And tired of selling tie clips, key rings, linen handkerchiefs, and manicure tools in little leather pouches. Gladys Ernestine had been with Conway's for forty-one years, forty-one years behind the tie counter.

"Just quit," Helen would say when Gladys complained. But with George gone, Gladys feared how long an afternoon at home might be. And she worried about how quickly her savings account might dwindle.

She was appalled at how little she had left in her checking account. Stopping at the bank machine on her lunch break, she had stared for a long time at the receipt the machine spit out.

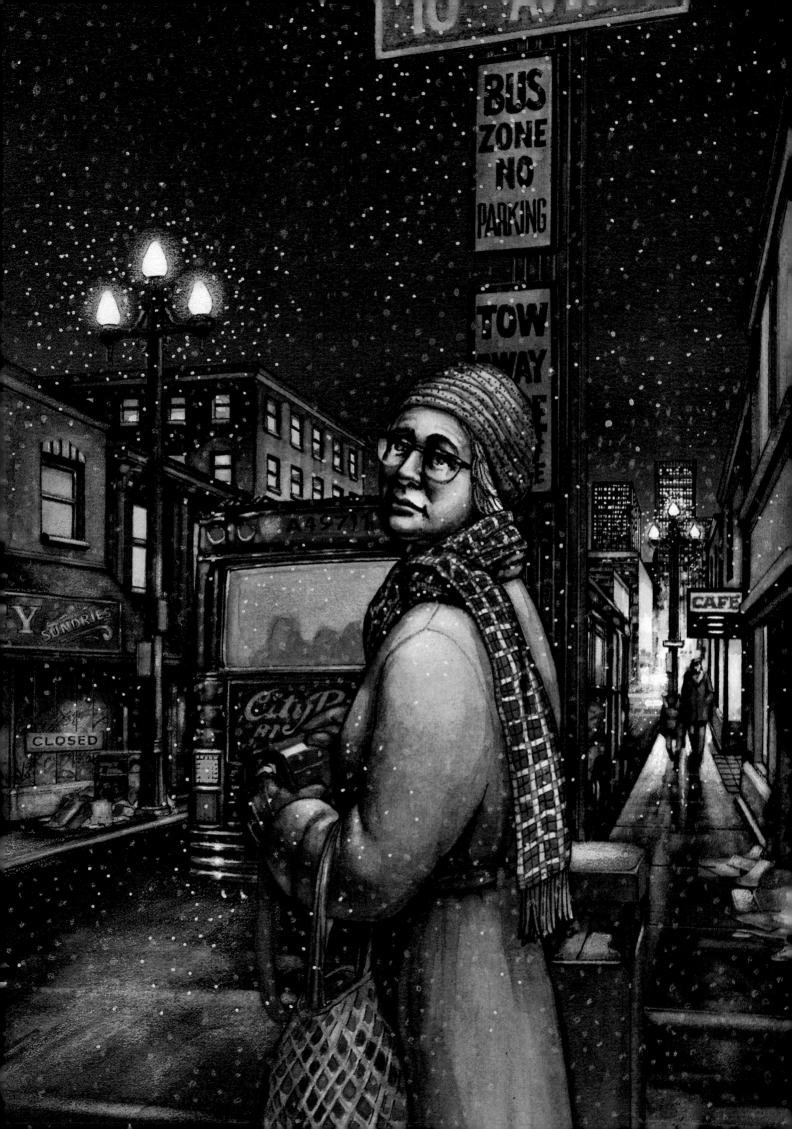

"Oh, my," she said, frowning. "Have I really spent that much this Christmas?"

A man called out from the line waiting behind her, "Hey, lady, you printing the stuff up there or what?"

She had finished her transaction, ignoring the rude stares of the people in line. Her mesh shopping bag hung from her wrist, limp and empty, filling her with a naggy, desperate feeling.

"I'll think of something to bring," she said. "I've got the whole afternoon."

Back at the store, Christmas music droned from the sound system, and customers crowded around the counter, annoyed with Gladys when she told them she had no more gift boxes.

"Send them over to shirts," Mr. Barth had said when she called up to the office.

"Those boxes are much too big for a tie."

"Then tell them to go buy a shirt to match the tie." He sounded as sour as the customers who stood glaring at her.

The afternoon dragged on. Gladys' feet hurt.

"What does it matter what I bring?" she mumbled at four o'clock as Mr. Barth began locking up the store. Gladys straightened the ties in the case and thought of George. He had been so easy to please. So like Father.

Then she remembered the stollen.

Father had discovered it.

Finally," Father had said, "a decent bakery in the neighborhood." He'd meant *German* bakery, of course. Weiss and Son, Bakers. Gladys had noticed the new sign as she walked to her parents' apartment one day.

They had all been just starting out then. Helen and Husband Number One, newly settled in their first house. Gladys and George, cozy in a small apartment over a florist's shop on Second Avenue. Even in winter, they could catch the sweet fragrance of roses.

They all came home that Christmas, back to the old neighborhood. After church, Father, in white shirt sleeves, his jacket hung on the back of his kitchen chair, cut the stollen. Helen made coffee. For once, their mother sat and let the others serve her. The stollen, sweet bread dense with fruit, was covered with confectioner's sugar. They licked their fingers and never thought to stop at only one piece.

"My mother made stollen just like this," Father said. "At Christmas. It was her gift to us."

As they ate, Helen chattered, telling stories about Gladys' first, flustered attempts at domesticity. "She calls me," Helen said, "and tells me, 'I don't understand what's wrong. I peeled the potatoes and cut them into French fries. I put them in the pan and the water is boiling, just like I've seen you do. But they're not turning brown.'" Helen laughed. "Can you imagine?"

Mother had smiled. "Oh, Gladys," she said, "you have to use oil."

George, touching her knee, had whispered, "That's okay. You've never let me starve yet."

Blushing, Gladys had raised her eyes to find her father's understanding smile on her. Although she had doubted it many times throughout her life, at that moment, Gladys felt absolutely certain of her father's love.

Once she remembered it, all Gladys could think of was stollen. As she filed out the employee door, people had called to her, "Merry Christmas." She barely heard them, her mind elsewhere, her heart craving Christmas stollen. She had boarded the bus, determined to find the old bakery and its stollen.

"How typical," she could hear Helen say, "Didn't it ever occur to you that the stollen was years ago? Weiss's Bakery is gone. And even if it weren't, no bakery would be open so late on Christmas Eve."

"I'll never tell her," Gladys said as she watched the back lights of the bus disappear into snowy darkness.

Suddenly, as she looked around, she was too frightened to feel foolish. A streetlight overhead cast an eerie glow through the snow. Stores lining the block were boarded up, their faded signs written in languages Gladys did not recognize. The old neighborhood was gone.

Up ahead, in the shadows, she spotted a man walking a dog. No one else was on the street. He moved quickly toward her. Gladys had never seen such a large dog. Gingerly, she stepped toward the curb. Perhaps a car, or a bus ahead of schedule might come by. She adjusted her glasses, hugged her purse, and wished herself invisible. The man and animal came closer, until they emerged from shadows into the circle of light from the streetlight. Gladys gasped. It was a donkey.

"Can you believe this?" the man said. He raised his hand, then placed it on his hip. His wool

overcoat was unbuttoned. Gladys noticed his tie, wondered where he'd bought it. Red paisley. Fine silk. Perfectly knotted. "It's his debut at St. Mark's Church," the man said, gesturing toward the animal. "We're already running late, and now he drops his blanket somewhere back there." The man gestured off into the darkness behind him. "Have you ever tried to stuff a jackass into a Volvo?"

"Oh, I don't have a car," Gladys said.

"Well, let me tell you, it does not fit."

The animal brayed.

"Sorry, my friend," he said, turning to look at the donkey, "but you've been nothing but trouble since Victor let me bring you down from the farm." The man raised his head and addressed the streetlight. "To think this was all my idea. 'Why, yes, Miss Perez, lovely brown-eyed choir director, I do know where I could get my hands on a donkey.' I must be crazy."

He looked at Gladys again. "Well? Will you help me?" He handed her the lead attached to the donkey's bridle. "I promise I'll be right back. Just let me find his blanket."

Before Gladys could protest, he stepped back into the shadows. "St. Mark's," she heard him call. "Just two blocks past the bus stop. I'll meet you there."

Gladys stared at the animal. His ears were twitching at the snow, his large eyes were calm. The man's voice came to her from farther away. "His name is Leopold."

"Leopold?" At the sound of his name, the donkey began to lead her away from the man and toward the church.

"No. Whoa, boy." The donkey plodded along. "Stop, I said." Her purse slid down her arm and slapped Leopold gently on his rump. He quickened his pace. "No. Heel." She was terrified of falling. "Please, stop, you miserable beast!"

They came to a street corner. Leopold ignored the red light and moved on. Gladys looked behind her to see if the man was coming. Snow and shadow curtained the bus stop. The animal's breath was visible. Snow had begun to stick to the pavement. Gladys relaxed her knees a bit, following the trail of hoof marks. Finally she saw a church.

A crowd had gathered on the front steps of the church under the illumination of lights set on top of tripods. Orange electrical cords ran from the lights down along the ground and around the corner of the building. An arc of people in choir robes stood around a manger. A woman portraying Mary, her nose red with cold, wore white mittens. She held a baby dressed in a bulky yellow snowsuit. Straw covered the church steps, and in a small pen by the manger stood two sheep and a goat. A little girl sat on the steps with a rabbit in her lap.

Leopold parted the crowd, and Gladys followed. "Miss Perez?" she said. A man pointed to a woman standing in front of the choir.

"Miss Perez, I brought your donkey." Gladys offered her the leather lead.

"Donkey?"

"The man back there. He said he'd bring you the donkey. He's on his way. As soon as he finds the blanket."

A man with a guitar stood next to Miss Perez. "We better get started," he said. "The baby is crying."

"I can't believe he actually found a donkey." Miss Perez smiled at Gladys.

"His name is Leopold," said Gladys.

The donkey moved again, leading Gladys close to the manger. The child fell silent when Leopold stopped in front of him.

"Nice donkey," said a man behind Gladys.

"Oh, he's not mine. I only came for stollen," Gladys said, turning toward the voice.

"Stollen?" The man chuckled. "You just came for the stollen, but you brought a donkey?" He chuckled again. "Well, it's downstairs. In the church hall."

Gladys faced a man her own age. "Really? Stollen? Here?"

"Yes. I make it every year for the party after the live nativity and concert."

The man wore a ski parka zipped up only halfway. Gladys noticed his tie. Wide and dated. Loosely knotted. The way George or any man who worked with his hands might wear a tie. George had been a welder.

"You make stollen?"

"Yes. My father, Rudolph Weiss, owned a bakery. For years. Just around the block. I still have friends at this church. It's nice to come back, especially every Christmas."

The child gurgled. Leopold bowed his head and ate straw. Gladys licked her lips, impatient to taste the stollen. She peered through the snow, wondering what she might do if the man with the red paisley tie never showed up. She chuckled at the thought of Leopold riding home on the bus with her. Leopold among the mahogany chairs in Helen's dining room. She felt a twinge of disappointment when she saw the man run up the church steps and wave to Miss Perez.

Cold wind billowed the shepherds' costumes and the choirs' robes. The music began. A quiet peace fell over Gladys, comforting as a father's loving smile.

Suddenly she was glad she had met the man with the donkey. How joyful it felt to stand in the chilly Christmas Eve night and listen to beautiful, ancient carols. How grand it was to be part of this wonderful nativity. Gladys reached out and gently patted Leopold's flank.

The next day at brunch, she had nothing to put on the table.

"Not even cranberry nut bread?" Helen said.

"I was out late last night." She tried to tell her sister the whole story. How she had met Leopold, the child in the snowsuit, the baker's son. How so many people had crowded into the church hall that by the time Gladys reached the table, only one piece of stollen was left.

"Are you crazy? Wandering around that part of the city at night? It's a miracle you weren't mugged. Or killed."

"No, Helen, that's not a miracle." Gladys reached in her pocket to reveal a small package wrapped in a paper napkin. She removed the napkin and held out a slice of Christmas stollen in both hands. "The miracle is I saved the last piece for you." 🐚

Bette Anne Gibson-Rieth lives in Shelton, Connecticut with her husband and two teenaged children. "'Christmas Stollen' began after I read about a live Nativity in New York City. Then, my mother-in-law told me how her mother made stollen every Christmas. Suddenly Gladys and Leopold took shape. The story is my response to the annual question, 'How can I make Christmas more meaningful?' The answer is simple: 'Return to the crèche.'"

Illustrator David Lund lives in Redmond, Washington and counts stollen at Christmastime among his own childhood memories.

Where Shepherds Lately Knelt

Jaroslav J. Vajda

Where shepherds lately knelt,
and kept the angel's word,
I come in half-belief,
a pilgrim strangely stirred;
but there is room
and welcome there
for me.

In that unlikely place
I find him as they said:
sweet newborn Babe, how frail!
and in a manger bed:
a still small Voice
to cry one day
for me.

How should I not have known
Isaiah would be there,
his prophecies fulfilled?
With pounding heart, I stare:
a Child, a Son,
the Prince of Peace—
for me.

Can I, will I forget
how Love was born and burned
its way into my heart—
unasked, unforced, unearned,
to die, to live,
and not alone
for me?

Jaroslav Vajda of St. Louis, Missouri, wrote this hymn
text for an earlier volume of *Christmas*. After choosing
a familiar subject—Jesus in the manger bed—Vajda
puzzled over how to give a fresh perspective to his
verses. He chose to picture himself visiting the
manger just after the shepherds had left.

Artist, illustrator, and teacher, Doree
Loschiavo of Philadelphia, Pennsylvania
has won many local and national
awards for her work. She strives to
capture the essence of energy
and color in her paintings.

Readings, Carols, Prayers, and Activities
Four Devotions for the
Christmas Season

Gather Around the Manger

D E B B I E   T R A F T O N   O ' N E A L

IS ANYTHING AS EXCITING AS THE CHRISTMAS SEASON? Delicious smells waft from ovens, joyful carols ring out over the radio, magical lights twinkle from tree branches. Christian homes around the world are getting ready for the birth of Jesus. Then, in the midst of all the bustle and fuss, a hush descends over the household: it's time to add the centerpiece to the celebration—the Christmas crèche.

The following worship suggestions use that centerpiece—the crèche—to help you recreate the story of Jesus' birth. The devotions are designed for use in homes, by families, during days before and after Christmas. If you're a family of one, why not invite friends or relatives to join you? Each devotion adds another piece to the crèche and another part to the Christmas story. By the time you've completed all four, you will have experienced the entire event of Christmas, complete with sights and sounds—even smells!— that can make the event truly memorable. The biblical story is printed out in speaking roles; so gather your "family" close, and let everyone take part in the reading.

1. THE STORY BEGINS

Preparations and Activities

Once you've chosen the best spot to assemble your crèche, the fun begins! Set up the stable (if you've got one) to one side of the area you've chosen. Place the figures of Mary, Joseph, and the donkey a short distance from the stable. Set up the shepherds and sheep some distance away.

Now create a unique background for your nativity scene—scenery that reflects the area where you live. If you live in a wooded area, for example, lay a flooring of moss or pine needles around the figures. If your home is in a desert region, use sand or pebbles. Palm leaves or Spanish moss can add color to southern crèche settings.

Next, place an empty manger into the stable. Near it, arrange a small pile of straw or hay. Part of the joy of Christmas is reaching out to other people. Tell family members that whenever they do a kind deed for someone, they should add a piece of straw to the manger. By Christmas morning, the manger should be filled with straw and ready for the Christ child!

As Christmas approaches, move the figures of Mary and Joseph progressively closer to the stable. By Christmas Eve, they should be next to the manger.

The Story   Luke 1:26-31; 2:1-7

NARRATOR: In the sixth month the angel Gabriel was sent by God to a town in Galilee called Nazareth, to a virgin engaged to a man whose name was Joseph, of the house of David. The virgin's name was Mary. And he came to her and said,

GABRIEL: "Greetings, favored one! The Lord is with you."

NARRATOR: But she was much perplexed by his words and pondered what sort of greeting this might be. The angel said to her,

GABRIEL: "Do not be afraid, Mary, for you have found favor with God. And now, you will conceive in your womb and bear a son, and you will name him Jesus."

NARRATOR: In those days a decree went out from Emperor Augustus that all the world should be registered. This was the first registration and was taken while Quirinius was governor of Syria. All went to their own towns to be registered. Joseph also went from the town of Nazareth in Galilee to Judea, to the city of David called Bethlehem, because he was descended from the house and family of David. He went to be registered with Mary, to whom he was engaged and who was expecting a child. While they were there, the time came for her to deliver her child. And she gave birth to her firstborn son and wrapped him in bands of cloth, and laid him in a manger, because there was no place for them in the inn.

Prayer

Lord of the day and the night, the sun and the moon, and all that lives and breathes on the earth: thank you for the gift of life that comes to us each morning when we awake. As we celebrate the wonderful gift you have given us in Jesus, your Son, help us always to remember to love others as you have loved us. Amen.

Carol   "Infant Holy, Infant Lowly" (*See page 21.*)

Gather Around the Manger

2. UNDER THE NIGHT SKY OF CHRISTMAS

Preparations and Activities

As the holy day approaches, close your eyes and imagine that first Christmas Eve. The sky is the darkest of blues, shadows are deep over the hills near Bethlehem. Suddenly the sky grows lighter and lighter as the stars try to outshine one another, and the air is filled with exquisite angel choirs singing "Hosanna in the highest!"

The night of nights is here. It is time to add the bright Bethlehem star to your nativity set. Also place an angel near the figures of shepherds and sheep.

When we think of the Christmas star and Christmas angels, we often picture shimmering gold and silver. Add these colors to your nativity set by stringing garlands of foil stars or by sprinkling glittering confetti around the crèche.

After this second section of the Christmas story has been read, move the shepherds and angel to the manger so they can view the miracle of God's birth.

The Story   Luke 2:8-20

NARRATOR: In that region there were shepherds living in the fields, keeping watch over their flock by night. Then an angel of the Lord stood before them, and the glory of the Lord shone around them, and they were terrified. But the angel said to them,

ANGEL: "Do not be afraid; for see—I am bringing you good news of great joy for all the people: to you is born this day in the city of David a Savior, who is the Messiah, the Lord. This will be a sign for you: you will find a child wrapped in bands of cloth and lying in a manger."

NARRATOR: And suddenly there was with the angel a multitude of the heavenly host, praising God and saying,

ANGELS: "Glory to God in the highest heaven, and on earth peace among those whom he favors!"

NARRATOR: When the angels had left them and gone into heaven, the shepherds said to one another,

SHEPHERDS: "Let us go now to Bethlehem and see this thing that has taken place, which the Lord has made known to us."

NARRATOR: So they went with haste and found Mary and Joseph, and the child lying in the manger. When they saw this, they made known what had been told them about this child; and all who heard it were amazed at what the shepherds told them. But Mary treasured all these words and pondered them in her heart. The shepherds returned, glorifying and praising God for all they had heard and seen, as it had been told them.

Prayer

Lord, we thank you for the good news you shared with shepherds on that first Christmas, and we thank you for the great Christmas news that we can share today with the people we know. Amen.

Carol   "Silent Night" (*See page 21.*)

3. FOLLOWING A STAR

Preparations and Activities

The magi, or wise men, are usually included in nativity scenes; but scholars believe that their visit took place some time later. No matter. The gifts of the wise men are an inspiration for Christmas gift-giving; these figures have a rightful place in the crèche. The January 6 celebration of Epiphany is when we remember the wise men, and their visit marks a close to the Christmas season. The following ideas can be used in the days after Christmas.

Add the figures of wise men and camels to the manger scene. In preparation for the biblical story, collect a small, scented candle; a piece of sandpaper cut into the shape of a path leading to the manger; and several cinnamon sticks.

Before the reading, light the candle. Then, as the story of the wise men is read, children can rub cinnamon sticks on the sandpaper path while moving the figures toward the manger. The wonderful scents will recall the gifts the magi offered the Christ child.

The Story   Matthew 2:1-12

NARRATOR: In the time of King Herod, after Jesus was born in Bethlehem of Judea, wise men from the East came to Jerusalem, asking,

WISE MEN: "Where is the child who has been born king of the Jews? For we observed his star at its rising, and have come to pay him homage."

NARRATOR: When King Herod heard this, he was frightened, and all Jerusalem with him; and calling together all the chief priests and scribes of the people, he inquired of them where the Messiah was to be born. They told him,

SCRIBES: "In Bethlehem of Judea; for so it has been written by the prophet: 'And you, Bethlehem, in the land of Judah, are by no means least among the rulers of Judah; for from you shall come a ruler who is to shepherd my people Israel.'"

NARRATOR: Then Herod secretly called for the wise men and learned from them the exact time when the star had appeared. Then he sent them to Bethlehem, saying,

HEROD: "Go and search diligently for the child; and when you have found him, bring me word so that I may also go and pay him homage."

NARRATOR: When they had heard the king, they set out; and there, ahead of them, went the star that they had seen at its rising, until it stopped over the place where the child was. When they saw that the star had stopped, they were overwhelmed with joy. On entering the house, they saw the child with Mary his mother; and they knelt down and paid him homage. Then, opening their treasure chests, they offered him gifts of gold, frankincense, and myrrh. And having been warned in a dream not to return to Herod, they left for their own country by another road.

Prayer

Lord, we thank you for the many gifts that you give us each day: our families, food to eat, and shelter against the evening air. But especially at this time of year, we thank you for the greatest gift of all—your Son, Jesus. Amen.

Carol   "Joy to the World" (*See page 21.*)

4. TRAVELING TO SAFETY

Preparations and Activities

Often, after Christmas Day has passed, we forget about our crèche and the story it depicts. But there is one final episode in the Christmas event. After the wise men had returned to their homes, Joseph was warned in a dream that the holy child was in danger. The family was to leave the land ruled by Herod and find a safer place to live.

Many lovely legends surround the family's flight to Egypt. A favorite tale describes how the family stopped to rest along the banks of a river. There, Mary took time to wash the cloths that wrapped baby Jesus, and spread them over a nearby bush to dry. After they had dried, Mary noticed that the cloths were as fragrant as the bush. "Ah," thought Mary, "I will name this bush Mary's Rose to remind me of its fragrance." When the infant reached out to touch the bush, small blue flowers burst forth from its branches. To this day, rosemary is a favorite Christmas herb.

If you can buy a live rosemary plant, place it near your nativity set, a reminder of the holy family's flight to safety. If you can't find a living plant, spread white glue over a small foam ball and roll it in dried rosemary. Push a pencil into the ball to make a topiary for your crèche. After reading the biblical story, share the legend of the rosemary and let family members and friends smell the sweet fragrance of the plant.

The Story   Matthew 2:13-15

NARRATOR: Now after they had left, an angel of the Lord appeared to Joseph in a dream and said,

ANGEL: "Get up, take the child and his mother, and flee to Egypt, and remain there until I tell you; for Herod is about to search for the child, to destroy him."

NARRATOR: Then Joseph got up, took the child and his mother by night, and went to Egypt, and remained there until the death of Herod.

Prayer

Lord, you provide everything that we need in this life, and you know all that we are afraid of. When we are unsure or afraid, remind us to trust in you to lead us just as you led Joseph and Mary and Jesus to safety. Amen.

Carol   "Let Our Gladness Have No End" 🎵

Let Our Gladness Have No End

Let our glad-ness have no end, Hal-le-lu-jah! For to earth did

Christ de-scend, Hal-le-lu-jah! *Refrain* On this day God gave us

Christ, his Son, to save us; Christ, his Son, to save us.

Infant Holy, Infant Lowly

In-fant ho-ly, in-fant low-ly, For his bed a cat-tle stall: Ox-en low-ing, lit-tle

know-ing Christ the child is Lord of all. Swift-ly wing-ing, an-gels sing-ing, Bells are

ring-ing, tid-ings bring-ing: Christ the child is Lord of all! Christ the child is Lord of all!

Silent Night

Si-lent night, ho-ly night! All is calm, all is bright Round yon

vir-gin moth-er and child. Ho-ly In-fant, so ten-der and mild,

Sleep in heav-en-ly peace, _____ Sleep in heav-en-ly peace.

Joy to the World

Joy to the world, the Lord is come! Let earth re-ceive its King; Let

ev-'ry heart pre-pare him room And heav'n and na-ture

sing, And heav'n and na-ture sing, And heav'n, and heav'n and na-ture sing.

Debbie Trafton O'Neal lives in Federal Way, Washington. She has always loved the story of Jesus' birth. "I remember as a child driving home from Christmas Eve services and watching for the brightest star in the sky. I was just sure God put it there to remind us of the star over the manger." Christmas has a special place in the life of her family. And there's an extra reason for them to celebrate: Christmas Day is also the birthday of Morgan Paige, one of three O'Neal daughters.

Illustrations by Viv Eisner-Hess, East Greenwich, Rhode Island.

One magical Christmas Eve, Papa Greccio gives his great-grandchildren three marvelous gifts: beautiful hand-carved nativity figures, a story of the first Christmas crèche, and a holiday tradition that will be cherished for generations.

A Christmas for Greccio

A READ-ALOUD STORY

BOB HARTMAN

PAPA GRECCIO SAT DOWN beside the tree and put a long finger to his lips. "Quiet now, children," he said, his accent untamed by eighty years in America. He bent over, picked up an old wooden crate, and set it on his lap. "Inside this box," he explained, "are some very special Christmas surprises. There is one for each of you. But you must promise not to open them until I say."

Then Papa Greccio passed out his surprises. They were wrapped in different colored tissue paper. They were small—no bigger than our hands. And they weighed hardly anything at all.

He passed them around to all his great-grandchildren—our cousins. And, last of all, he gave one to each of us.

"For Maria," he smiled, handing me a blue one.

"For Sarah." He gave my younger sister a gift wrapped in green.

"And finally," he said, as the light from the lamp caught his bald head and bright eyes, "one for young John."

My little brother took the last surprise in his five-year-old hands and stared at it like it was a gift from God himself. "What's in it, Maria?" he whispered.

"Just wait," I answered. "Papa Greccio will tell you when to open it."

Papa Greccio sat back down. He ran that bony finger across his thin, white mustache. Then, slowly and mysteriously, he began.

"Tonight is Christmas Eve. And that is what this story is about: a Christmas Eve long ago, in a little village in Italy called Greccio—the village where our family got its name."

"Like Papa Greccio!" shouted John.

"That's right," smiled the old man. "Now, listen: Greccio sat on a wooded hill across the valley from Mount Terminillo. On the rocky slope of that mountain there were caves. And in one of those caves, a holy man named Francis built a little church."

Papa Greccio took the wooden crate from his lap, turned it on its side, and placed it on the platform under the tree. Then he asked my cousin Joe to unwrap his surprise. Inside was the carved figure of a man with his arms stretched out and upward—and a little bird was perched on his shoulder.

"Perhaps you have heard of this Francis," continued Papa Greccio. And he took the figure from Joe and set it next to the box. "He was a saint—a man chosen by God to do special things. Francis rebuilt broken-down churches, helped poor, broken-down people, and traveled across this broken-down world talking about God's love. And his voice and his life were so pure that even the animals stopped to listen to him.

"He kept nothing for himself and claimed that his only goal was to walk in the footsteps of his master, Jesus. And some say that Francis came closer than any other man to doing just that.

"Anyway, it was this same Francis who decided to do something special for the people in Greccio that Christmas long ago. He called together his friends—the Little Brothers—and told them to bring him . . . well . . . Sarah, if you will unwrap your parcel, we can see for ourselves."

My sister carefully pulled apart the tissue paper. And inside, she found . . .

"A manger! It's a little wooden manger filled with straw." And she took it to Papa Greccio just like the Little Brothers took their manger to Francis.

Papa Greccio set the manger in the middle of the crate and returned to his tale.

"But that wasn't all that Francis asked the Little Brothers to bring. No indeed. He meant to make something that would look as much like that first Christmas as possible. So he asked another of his friends to bring what Carl has in his surprise, and another to bring . . . let's see . . . what I have given to Louisa!"

As soon as their names were called, my cousins started unwrapping.

"A donkey!" called Carl.

"And a cow!" said Louisa.

They set the animals on either side of the little manger.

Papa Greccio smiled and nodded. "Now the Little Brothers were sent down the mountain and across the valley to fetch the villagers. So I suppose that all of you with brown parcels need to unwrap them."

On cue, Gina and Theresa and Andrew and James and all three of the triplets tore into their packages and produced a whole collection of little men in long robes with half-shaved heads. Some were walking, some were running or jumping, and one was holding a little pig!

"And now, the yellow parcels," added Papa Greccio.

After more ripping and tearing, out came the carved villagers: a boy with a stick, a little girl, a baker and a blacksmith and a fat old woman. A jester and a juggler and a soldier. A tall man on a horse with a fine lady beside him. There was a crippled woman, too, and a beggar and a priest. I was glad that we had such a big family, for I would not have wanted to miss any of these villagers.

"And so the entire village came," continued Papa Greccio, "and stood with the Little Brothers before the manger." Then he called us forward and, one by one, the figures were set in place.

John turned to me, teary-eyed. "I want to open mine, Maria. Why can't I open mine?"

"Just wait," I told him. "I haven't opened mine yet, either. We'll get our turn, I'm sure."

"Now you may wonder," said Papa Greccio, "how did the villagers find their way? It was dark, after all. It was nearly midnight on the darkest day of the year."

Then he paused and reached behind him. "They brought torches—that is how. And the sky was lit with stars!"

As soon as he'd said those words, he threw a switch and the Christmas tree burst bright with lights. There were lights on the platform beneath the tree, too, flickering like torches among the carved figures. We ooohed and ahhhed; we blinked and pointed.

When everything was quiet again, Papa Greccio went on. "Then Francis stepped forward and sang for them—from the Gospels—the story of the first Christmas. We don't know how the tune went, but we do know that the poor people of Greccio wept when they heard how God had used a poor, young woman—poorer even than themselves—to bring his love into the world."

And that is when Papa Greccio called to me. "Maria, open your parcel and bring it here."

Even before I undid the paper, I knew what was inside. My namesake—her head bowed, on her knees, her hands folded in prayer.

"It's Mary!" said John. "She's pretty."

I could only nod my head and agree.

Then I set her behind the manger, next to where my cousin Thomas had already placed a tall, wooden Joseph.

"Finally," Papa Greccio concluded, "everyone began to sing. Francis and the Little

Brothers and the villagers joined their voices and filled the cave with song. And, so, I think we should sing now, too."

"Wait!" called my brother. "Wait, Papa Greccio! I want to open my present."

Papa Greccio sat back, straight and tall. Then he snapped his fingers. "Of course. How could I have forgotten? The most important part of the story is yet to come." And he called my little brother to his side.

"Did you know there was a knight at this Christmas celebration?" he asked.

"You mean the kind that fights dragons?" said John.

"Perhaps," answered Papa Greccio. "He was certainly rich and powerful—that is, until he met Francis. Then he gave up his riches and his knighthood to live in poverty and do good works. Do you know what this knight's name was?"

My brother shook his head.

"His name was Giovanni. That is Italian . . . for John.

"Well, this knight—John—heard the music and the story, and he saw the lights and the manger like everyone else who was there. But he saw something else, as well—something nobody else saw. And if you unwrap your present, John, you will see it, too."

Slowly and carefully, my little brother unfolded the tissue paper. No one else made a sound. It was surely the quietest my cousins had ever been. And when he had unwrapped his gift, John showed it to nobody. He simply handed it to Papa Greccio.

And Papa Greccio laid it in the manger.

"A miracle? A vision? Who knows?" said Papa Greccio very quietly. "But when the crowd heard that the knight Giovanni had seen the Child of Bethlehem, the cave, the valley—even Mount Terminillo itself—could not contain the joy or the songs of praise that followed!"

And so we sang, too. We, and our parents around us, and our grandparents, and our great-grandfather singing loudest of all: *Adeste Fideles, Away in a Manger, Hark! The Herald Angels Sing.*

When the crowd heard that the knight had seen the Child of Bethlehem, even Mount Terminillo itself could not contain the joy that followed.

That was a long time ago, now. Papa Greccio died the following spring. And at his funeral, we cousins made ourselves a promise.

Every year, from cities and towns and villages all across this country and this world, we come together. We bring the figures he carved for us. We tell the story. We light the lights. Our children open the presents and set them underneath the tree.

And there is Christmas at Greccio again. 🖋

Bob Hartman is a writer, minister, and professional storyteller from Ben Avon, Pennsylvania. Born and raised in multi-ethnic Pittsburgh, Bob has a deep appreciation for the cultural traditions and sense of family that hold so many ethnic groups together. "A Christmas for Greccio" is his tribute to those communities and to the faith they share.

Artist Lee M. Steadman of McKean, Pennsylvania thought of his own family as he created the watercolor illustration for this story: "The most special moments to me are those spent sitting around a sparkling Christmas tree sharing jokes, stories, and memories from times past with my family and children. It is during such moments that time seems to stop and we enjoy what is most important of all."

The National Museum of Bavaria is home to a collection
of priceless Christmas treasures—
over two hundred of the most magnificent nativity scenes ever created.

The Nativity in Miniature

NAN BAUROTH

EVERY YEAR THEY TAKE CENTER STAGE on our mantels and under our Christmas trees: Mary, Joseph, the baby Jesus, and near them in the stable, the ox and ass. Humble shepherds soon join the cast, trailed by turbaned Moors and a host of hovering angels. In a few magical moments, our homes are transformed into backdrops for the most dramatic pageant the world has ever known.

The nativity scene, as this miniature theatrical production is known, has been around for centuries. The Germans call it *krippe*, the French, *crèche*. Italians refer to it as *praesepe*, the Spanish, *nacimiento*. Popularized by southern Europeans, nativity scenes have become a standard holiday fixture in Christian homes all over the globe.

It was St. Francis of Assisi who introduced the *praesepe* as a way to dramatize the birth of Christ. In 1224, inspired by the sight of shepherds tending their flocks in the moonlight, Francis asked a wealthy friend from the town of Greccio to help him construct a live manger scene, complete with ox and ass. On Christmas Eve, townspeople came in droves to gaze in awe at the lifelike reproduction of God's arrival on earth.

Not surprisingly, word of the dramatization at Greccio spread, and the idea caught on. By the fifteenth century, nativity scenes proliferated in monasteries and churches throughout southern Europe. Officials saw these as a way to teach people the stories of the Bible, literally bringing the Scriptures to life.

Several hundred years later, nativity scenes had become an art form. Eminent sculptors, artists, and jewelers created miniature masterpieces to indulge royalty and aristocrats. In keeping with artistic sentiments of the time, figures became increasingly realistic, while sets grew more intricate and more spectacular, incorporating the latest scientific and technological inventions.

A penchant for grandiosity in nativity scenes may have originated in Naples, where early *praesepes* appeared on rooftops of the wealthy upper classes. The German poet Goethe described these life-sized stagings: "The mother of God, the child, the whole retinue and following is elaborately fitted up, the clothes costing the household a great deal of money. But what makes it all so inimitable is the background dominated by Vesuvius and its surroundings."

Eventually nativity scenes, or "cribs," moved from the rooftop into the house, and the craze for miniature cribs was born. Charles of Bourbon, who took the crown of Naples in 1734, encouraged this mania by carving his own figures, which were then arrayed in royal clothing by his wife. Legend has it that other European queens, caught up in a religious frenzy, would doff their finery to provide gowns for the dolls.

The church kept an uneasy eye on the growing fascination with nativity scenes. In 1780, concerned that its flock had gone astray, the church banned many colorful religious customs, including nativity scenes. The ban remained in effect for nearly a hundred years, but it only encouraged the common people, who had come to love Christmas cribs, to carve their own figures and set them up secretly in their homes. This cottage industry flourished especially in the alpine regions of Bavaria and Tyrol.

Perhaps the finest collection of cribs (*krippen*) is housed in Munich's National Museum of Bavaria. On display are over two hundred of the most magnificent cribs ever created, the gift of Munich banker Max Schmederer, who devoted his life to collecting and preserving these works of art.

As a boy, Schmederer was often ill and confined to his house. One Christmas, his parents gave him a nativity scene to occupy his long and solitary days. Schmederer was entranced with the gift and spent endless hours playing with the tiny figures. As he grew older, he began collecting Christmas cribs, often creating elaborate landscape settings for them.

A generous man, Schmederer opened his home each year at Christmas so that families throughout the city of Munich could enjoy his hobby. By 1895, the crowds had grown so large that he decided to donate his collection to the Bavarian National Museum. Every year until his death in 1917, he helped stage the display for the annual Christmas exhibit the citizens of Munich had come to love.

The Annunciation

Today the Krippen Exhibit is open year-round, and people from all over the world come to tour the spectacular display of antique nativity scenes. On entering, you pass into an anteroom of glass cases containing early dolls of the infant Jesus. These models of the holy child originated in medieval convents where young girls were cloistered by their families at the tender age of twelve.

As you leave this anteroom, the lights dim and you are transported magically to another time and place, to witness an event that changed the world. In the rooms of Schmederer's collection, cribs of various sizes and settings are grouped to reflect events in the biblical storyline.

Dr. Nina Gockerell, curator of the Krippen Exhibit, explains that by definition, the Christmas crib is a movable feast. "The crib must be made up of figures that are independent of each other. It must be possible to change the scenery, to tell the whole story from the Annunciation to the Flight into Egypt. The crib is like a stage where you move the actors around."

ONE OF THE MOST POPULAR ANNUNCIATION CRIBS depicts a humble Mary kneeling on a cushion as an angel descends with the startling news. The dramatic and fluid effect of the angel's gown is characteristic of Neapolitan artists' flair for action and lifelike figurines.

PROGRESSING THROUGH THE EXHIBIT, you encounter "The Search for the Inn," which shows an exhausted and disheartened Mary watching as an unfriendly innkeeper turns Joseph away. The Palestinian dress on the characters in the foreground reflects the Eastern influence on costume designers during this period. The puppets in this crib are made of wood, the work of Munich carvers in the nineteenth century.

The museum has a wealth of extraordinary cribs which depict the nativity as if it had taken place in the artists'

The Search for the Inn

native lands. In one scene, Tyroleans sporting embroidered lederhosen ascend an alpine peak in search of the Christ child; in another, Venetian gondoliers in ribboned hats crowd a marketplace, flirting with peasant girls while toting baskets of grapes bound for the wine press.

"THE SHEPHERDS' OFFERING" is one of the more reverential stagings of the nativity event. In this scene, Schmederer sets the birth in a gloomy, windowless vestibule beneath a vaulted Roman arch. An ox and ass watch over the infant as shepherds offer gifts of fruit and lambs to the holy family.

A WONDERFULLY BREATHTAKING SCENE, "The Shepherds in the Field," illustrates a "new" approach to crib design that evolved at the beginning of the twentieth century. Figures in earlier nativity scenes were dressed in the native costumes of the artisans—Tyrolean, Bavarian, Neapolitan, etc. Increased travel to the Middle East excited an interest in more realistic Palestinian dress. In this scene, the herdsmen appear in sandals and tunics amidst the arid hills of Judea. Of special note are the fighting bulls and flock of grazing sheep carved by master Bavarian artisans.

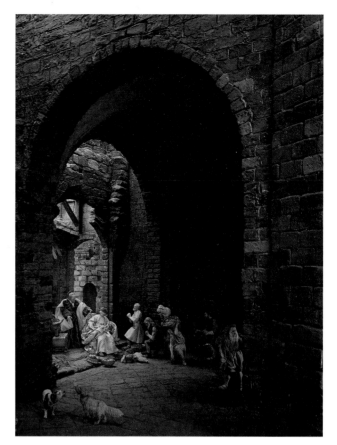

The Shepherds' Offering

The Shepherds in the Field

The Procession of the Three Kings

"THE PROCESSION OF THE THREE KINGS" captures the visit of the magi in a grand and elegant panorama. Enthroned on a jewel-studded elephant, an exotic Eastern monarch parades through the desert, preceded by royal guards on prancing Arabian steeds. The opulent garments and finely carved heads on these figures mark them as extremely valuable. This magnificent crib is an important example of Bavarian style of the 1800s, which featured lavish sets and costumes rich in Eastern detail.

As you wander from one display to another, you will be struck by the remarkable realism of the tiny figures. Their natural poses, animated gestures, and expressive faces make them seem almost frozen in time. Artisans achieved this effect by constructing the bodies of tow and wire, thereby making each figure pliable and allowing its stance to be changed at will. Arms and legs were shaped of finely carved wood; heads were fashioned from wax, porcelain, or terra-cotta, which was then painted.

The backdrops, many of which Schmederer designed, are works of art in their own right.

These spectacular biblical landscapes make you feel as if you were actually present at the momentous events. The sands stretch endlessly into a timeless horizon, the star of Bethlehem shines so clearly and magically that you feel yourself being drawn into the ancient quest of the wise men.

No matter how splendid and varied the backdrops, costuming, or design of the cribs, however, one thing remains constant in all the scenes: rich and poor folk alike come to worship the Son of God. In these miniature stagings, kings and queens rub shoulders with the lowliest peasants, a reminder that, in the presence of the Christ child, all are equal.

The significance of the Christmas crib was beautifully expressed by St. Francis upon seeing the effects of the manger scene he had created: "Thus Simplicity was honored, Poverty exalted, Humility commended, and . . . there was made, as it were, a new Bethlehem." 🪶

Photographs courtesy of the Bayerisches National Museum, Munich, Germany. Used by permission.

Nan Bauroth fell in love with the Krippen Exhibit while on holiday in Bavaria in 1980. A former marketing executive for a national financial group, she lives in Charlotte, North Carolina, where she now serves as a marketing consultant and writes books about the criminal mind.

Crèche

VALERIE WORTH

The sheep
Tend to
Fall over,

The angel
Is lacking
A wing;

Even the
Baby looks
Shabby—

So that
It's hard
To explain

Their sturdy
Abiding
Beauty.

From *At Christmastime*. (Michael de Capua Books, San Francisco: HarperCollins Publishers, 1992). Copyright © 1992 Valerie Worth. Used by permission of HarperCollins Publishers.

Author and poet Valerie Worth won numerous awards for her children's poetry. Her brief poems present fresh visions that lead readers to appreciate the uniqueness and wonder in ordinary things.

Illustration by Mary Worcester, Wayzata, Minnesota.

What did a lonely, middle-aged widow know about buying gifts for anonymous eleven-year-old girls? When she enlists the help of her feisty young neighbor, Jeanne learns more about adolescents— and about friendship—than she'd bargained for.

That Christmas Feeling

LYNEA BOWDISH

EANNE PRETENDED to be looking at the Christmas cards displayed on the rack in Milton's Pharmacy. Out of the corner of her eye she studied the nearby tree. The tree was covered in white tags tied with red string. In another week most of the tags would be gone, each replaced with a brightly wrapped package on the floor beneath the tree. She wondered what happened to the children whose tags weren't chosen.

Jeanne took a deep breath, straightened her shoulders, and marched up to the tree. Her eyes scanned the tags. "Girl—10 months." "Boy—age 2." "Boy—3 months."

She'd choose a baby. A girl. A baby would be easy to buy a gift for—something to wear, a toy, a stuffed animal, a rattle.

Here and there on the tree's branches were tags for older children. Her eyes came to rest on one of these: "Girl—age 11." Jeanne stared at the tag and frowned. She knew nothing about eleven-year-old girls.

With a sudden movement, she lifted a tag off the tree, jammed it in her pocketbook, and headed for the door before she could change her mind.

Once in the car, she took the tag out and looked at it.

"Girl—age 11."

What did a 56-year-old woman with one unmarried son know about a gift for an eleven-year-old girl? Jeanne sighed. But she knew why she had chosen this tag. Babies were appealing; their tags were sure to be taken. The tags that weren't chosen were those of the older children. Left behind and forgotten.

Like her.

It was no good to give in to self-pity. The Christmas blues, she called it, but she knew the feeling had been around for a long time. Christmas only made it a little worse. This would be her third Christmas since Tom had died. She should be getting used to it by now. But her son Jack was in Germany for the second Christmas in a row. And what was left of her family—her brother and cousins—were all in Maine, which was a long way from Maryland.

Girl—age 11. She certainly was not going to put the tag back. She'd figure out something to buy.

When Jeanne pulled into her driveway, she heard the beat of loud music from the house next door. Lacey was home.

A sudden inspiration struck her. Lacey must be about ten or eleven by now; she might have an idea about a suitable gift.

Jeanne slipped out of the car and crossed the lawn to the Evans' house. She knocked on the door, loudly. After several seconds, the music was turned down; then a young girl in jeans and a baggy black tee shirt opened the door. She pushed her long brown hair back with one hand and peered at Jeanne.

"My mother's left for work."

Jeanne knew Mrs. Evans, a nurse, worked the evening shift at the hospital.

"It's you I wanted to see, Lacey," Jeanne said.

"Why?" The girl didn't sound rude, just curious. Jeanne quickly explained.

"You want me to help you pick out a present?"

Lacey stared at her in surprise. "For someone you've never met?"

Having Lacey go with her to pick out a present wasn't really what Jeanne had in mind, but it might work. And Jeanne needed help.

"I thought, since you were about her age . . ."

"I'm twelve," Lacey said, raising her chin. "I'll be thirteen in June."

"Yes, well, that's even better," Jeanne said. "Then you're sure to know what she'd like, since you've already been eleven." Jeanne smiled at her little attempt at humor, but Lacey didn't seem to notice it.

"I'll think about it," Lacey said, and closed the door.

Jeanne blinked at the closed door, the smile still on her face. Well, that was abrupt. Then she turned and walked across to her own house. Lacey and her parents had moved in five years earlier, before Tom had died. And although Tom had talked to Mrs. Evans occasionally when he was working in the yard, Jeanne had never gotten to know her or her daughter. She was vaguely aware that the husband had moved out nearly a year ago. What was his name, anyway? From a distance she had seen the child grow up, watching as Lacey got taller, noticing that babysitters had stopped coming to stay with her.

Jeanne hung her coat in the closet and glanced into the living room on her way into the kitchen. The tree stood where she had put it the day after Thanksgiving.

Determined to acknowledge Christmas this year, she had assembled the artificial tree and placed it in the corner by the front window, where it had always stood when Tom was alive. There it remained with nothing on it, not even lights. It was one week until Christmas, and she knew she'd do nothing more with the tree. At least this year she had put it up.

Jeanne went into the kitchen and sat at the table. She pulled the tag from her pocketbook and stared at it. Toys, maybe? No, she'd be too old for toys. Clothes? Jeanne had hated getting clothes for Christmas when she was a child. Jewelry? Makeup? Did girls of eleven use makeup? Jeanne sighed deeply. She had never bothered with this sort of thing before. Why now?

Maybe she needed to feel again the fun of buying Christmas presents. The ones to Germany had been sent off in a big box in October, and those to Maine had been mailed before Thanksgiving. It hadn't even felt like Christmas back then. It didn't feel like Christmas now either.

No Christmas feeling at all.

That's what she had called it when she was a child—"that Christmas feeling." The excitement and anticipation down deep in her stomach. She'd never known when it would arrive—maybe when she was talking about Christmas with her friends, or shopping with her mother, or rehearsing for the Sunday school Christmas pageant—but it had always come, and it had stayed with her through the holidays. She didn't remember when it had stopped coming. One year it wasn't there, and she'd never had it again. Maybe it had stopped the year her father died. She'd been about Lacey's age.

Jeanne sighed again. Enough thoughts about Christmas for one day. She'd think about a gift for "Girl—age 11" tomorrow.

> ## "That Christmas feeling" ... One year it wasn't there, and she'd never had it again.

When Lacey showed up at the door the next afternoon, Jeanne was surprised.

"I've come about the present," Lacey said.

The girl swept past her and walked into the living room.

"Your tree's not decorated," Lacey pointed out.

Jeanne wondered if she was always this abrupt—almost rude—or if the girl's strange behavior was a sign of something else. Maybe she was on drugs. Jeanne stifled a laugh. Drugs! What did she know about drugs? She'd never heard that drugs made people abrupt.

"Please sit down," Jeanne said. "Did you come up with an idea for the gift?"

"Not really," Lacey said. She looked around the room, avoiding Jeanne's eyes, then sat down on the arm of the couch. "I thought maybe we could go to Reed's and look."

Reed's was a huge department store about forty-five minutes from the house. Jeanne hadn't been there since before Tom died, making do with smaller local stores. She hesitated. She was missing something here.

"What about someplace closer?" Jeanne suggested, studying Lacey's face.

The girl still didn't look at her. Her eyes were fixed on the naked tree.

"My father took me to Reed's once. It just seemed like the kind of place we could find something. But never mind. It doesn't matter."

Lacey got up as if to leave.

"No, no. Reed's will be fine," Jeanne said. "Tell me about the store. I haven't been there since my son was a teenager."

"It's great," Lacey said, sitting back down with a quick motion. "They have lots of clothes and jewelry and makeup, and downstairs in the basement is a bakery where you can buy things just made and eat them right there—" She broke off suddenly.

"Of course that's not what you want to do. But all the kids at school go to Reed's, and they talk about the clothes and stuff . . ." She settled back, slipping down into the couch, all animation going out of her.

"It sounds like you and your father had a good time," Jeanne said. Was she being too obvious? Would the girl think she was prying?

Lacey continued staring at the tree. "Yeah, we had a good time." She gave a small sigh and shrugged her shoulders. "When my mother wasn't along. When she was, they'd argue and fight and everyone would stare."

She glanced quickly at Jeanne, as if to see if she'd said too much. Then, embarrassed, she looked back at the tree.

"Tom—my husband—and I argued sometimes," Jeanne said, trying to fill the silence. "I hated it when we did. But after he died, I missed it." Her eyes followed Lacey's to the empty tree. "I missed having somebody around to fight with."

Lacey turned and stared at her with wide eyes.

"I know," she said. "Sometimes I think I'd rather have them fighting than not have him around."

Lacey suddenly stood up. "Well, do you want to go?"

Jeanne felt lost for a moment. Evidently Lacey had changed the subject. The store! That must be it.

"I think it's a good idea," Jeanne said. "The trip to Reed's, I mean. How about Saturday? I have to deliver the present to the store on Monday. They distribute the gifts on Christmas Eve."

"OK," Lacey said. "My mother works Saturday and Sunday nights, so she sleeps all day. I don't have anything else to do."

Embarrassed again, she added, "I could always hang out with my friends. I mean, there's plenty to do . . ."

"Saturday then," Jeanne said. She was getting uncomfortable with Lacey's worries about revealing too much. "About eleven? Maybe we can have lunch there, too."

Lacey's eyes lit up, but she quickly looked back to the tree.

"I guess so," she said, trying to sound unenthusiastic. "You really ought to get that tree decorated. It doesn't even have lights. I put ours up the week before Thanksgiving."

She turned abruptly and headed for the door. "But suit yourself," she said. "See you Saturday."

She was gone before Jeanne had a chance to say goodbye.

Saturday was clear and cold. Jeanne found that in the moving car, with something to focus on besides each other, conversation came easier. Her first impressions didn't change, however. Lacey seemed lonely, and the girl missed her father more than she admitted.

"My father and I always put the tree up together," Lacey explained. "And in plenty of time, so we'd be able to enjoy it. We'd sit at night with only the tree lights on and look at it and talk together."

"I miss my family most at Christmas time," Jeanne said.

Lacey stared out the side window. "I didn't know older people got lonely. My mother never seems to."

Jeanne heard the word with a start. Lonely. Was that what she was? She knew that she missed Tom. Missed him desperately. But she'd never thought of herself as lonely.

The parking place they finally found was far from the entrance to Reed's, and Jeanne had to hurry to keep up with Lacey's long, eager strides. Inside, they paused to look up at the green trees mounted high above the crowds. The trees were covered with white satin bows and twinkling white lights. Below them, counters sparkled with smaller trees in green and white. In the background, bells played Christmas carols.

They walked up and down the crowded aisles, and after much looking and considering, chose a bracelet and a big tee-shirt for Girl—age 11.

"It won't matter what size she is," Lacey explained. "The shirt's supposed to look big. And she can always tuck it in."

Then, because they both automatically stopped at the perfume counter display to sniff some of the sample scents, they added a small bottle of light perfume.

"I used to wear this when I was her age," Lacey said, as if it had been years ago. She pushed her hair back with her hand. "You don't want to get anything too old for her, like what I wear now sometimes."

Jeanne looked at the girl in amazement. She hadn't realized that this awkward, abrupt adolescent dressed in jeans and baggy shirt would even consider wearing perfume.

Next they stopped to admire rings. Lacey tried on a silver band with a small pearl.

"My birthstone is pearl. For June." She held out her hand so the pearl would catch the light. "My father bought me nice things sometimes," she said. "Mother does, too," she added quickly. "But you know how it is—money is money . . . Come on, I'll show you the bakery."

Jeanne, now used to the sudden changes in topic, followed Lacey to the escalator. The aroma of baked goods floated up to meet them as they descended. Jeanne left Lacey wandering along the counters while she went to the bathroom. Then she raced back to the first floor for that pearl ring.

A thank you, Jeanne said to herself. She'd make it a Christmas present.

Back downstairs, Lacey was studying an eclair. They each ate one as they sat at a small wire table in a corner decorated to look like an outdoor Paris cafe. Then they went next door to have lunch.

"After all," Jeanne said, "we've had dessert. We might as well have lunch."

This time Lacey laughed at the small joke, and Jeanne realized how good it felt to hear that sound coming from her.

Later they drove home in friendly silence, neither having the energy to talk.

That night Jeanne couldn't sleep. She blamed it on her legs, tired from so much walking. She hadn't spent a whole day shopping in years. But her thoughts kept wandering back to Lacey.

On Monday morning Jeanne wrapped the presents for Girl—age 11, put them into a large box, and took them to the store. She put the package under the tree and left quickly.

That afternoon, Lacey was at her door as soon as the school bus dropped her off.

"I came to help wrap the presents," Lacey announced, walking past Jeanne and into the living room. "I remember you said we had to get them over to the store today. Christmas Eve is tomorrow."

Jeanne felt her stomach sink.

"Lacey, I'm sorry." Jeanne clasped her hands together. "I already wrapped them. I dropped them off at the store this morning."

Lacey stared at her, and her mouth dropped open. Then she turned away and stared at the tree.

"That tree looks awful," she said. "Why did you put it up if you weren't going to decorate it? Is that how you do things? Make promises and then forget them?"

The girl's voice rose, but she still didn't look at Jeanne. "That's okay. I really don't care. You needed me for something. I helped you out. Good. Fine. Fair enough."

She whirled and stared at Jeanne. And this time she nearly yelled.

"Couldn't we have finished it together?" Lacey pushed her hair back with a trembling hand. "Couldn't you have waited? Did you have to forget about me? Didn't it ever occur to you to think about me a little?"

Lacey had changed the topic again, but this time Jeanne had no trouble keeping up with her.

She wasn't talking only about Jeanne now. Jeanne's eyes filled, and she stretched out her hand to the girl, but Lacey pushed past her, and in a moment the door slammed behind her.

Jeanne stood in the middle of the floor, tears streaming down her face. What was wrong with her? A grown woman this upset simply because a neighbor child had a tantrum over a small disappointment?

She collapsed into a chair and stared at the bare tree. She hadn't thought it meant that much. She hadn't *thought*; that was the problem. She'd been too caught up in her own feelings—yes, in her own loneliness. She had asked Lacey to help her solve a problem and then left the girl out of the resolution.

Jeanne didn't sleep that night either. She hadn't known anything about what to buy for Girl—age 11; and she'd known less than nothing about being a friend to a girl, age twelve. Almost thirteen.

The next day, Jeanne watched from her window as Lacey's mother left in the afternoon for work. When the mail carrier had passed, Jeanne slipped on her jacket, picked up the small package she had wrapped in red and green, and took it next door. It was small enough to fit on top of the mail in the mailbox. The beat of loud music came from inside.

She hurried home in the cold air. Whatever Lacey thought of her, she had at least delivered the present. There would at least be this small thank-you.

The afternoon dragged into evening. It was Christmas Eve. Jeanne wondered whether to go to the eight o'clock church service or wait for the eleven o'clock carol service. The carol service had always been Tom's favorite. Even when Jack was a baby, they'd bundled him up—sleeping peacefully—and carried him along to the service. It had always seemed like they were really ready for Christmas as they stepped out of church into the crisp midnight air. It had been years since she'd attended that eleven o'clock service.

Jeanne pulled out the box of lights, hoping to work up some enthusiasm to put them on the tree. But all she could do was sit and stare at the bare tree. Lacey had been right. She was lonely. She didn't let people into her life anymore. She didn't go places or do things that she used to enjoy. She was as bare and empty as that tree.

The doorbell rang.

Lacey was standing outside, wrapped in a big blue jacket.

"Hello," the girl said.

When Jeanne didn't answer, Lacey shrugged and walked past her into the living room. Jeanne followed her slowly.

"I've come to put the lights on the tree. You can't leave it like that."

> She'd known less than nothing about being a friend to a girl, age twelve. Almost thirteen.

The girl dropped her jacket on a chair, pushed her hair back with one hand, and plopped to the floor next to the box of lights. As she began pulling strands out of the box, the lamplight caught the sparkle of the small silver ring with the white pearl.

Lacey saw Jeanne looking at the ring, and the girl's face deepened with color.

"I guess you did think of me after all," Lacey said. Then, in her usual abrupt style, added: "Are you going to help me with this or not?"

Jeanne took the end of the string of lights from Lacey, and their hands brushed each other.

Jeanne smiled. Maybe, after they got the tree decorated, they could have some cookies and hot chocolate. And maybe she'd ask Lacey to go with her to the eleven o'clock church service. It would be nice to hear the carols again. Nice to have someone with her to share them.

Somewhere, down deep in her stomach, Jeanne felt the beginnings of something she hadn't felt for years. It used to come earlier in the season, she recalled.

But better late than never. ✍

Lynea Bowdish, of Hollywood, Maryland, writes: "As a former college teacher who has also worked with senior citizens and who writes for children, I have always been fortunate to have friends of many ages. Those who gathered at the manger were people of various occupations, ages, and visions. Christmas is a time to reach out across backgrounds and generations. In touching each other, we renew the Christmas spirit in ourselves."

Artist David Danz lives in Pasadena, California with his wife and four children. In addition to his work as a woodcut, linocut, and scratchboard illustrator, he plays guitar and leads a children's choir as a part of his church's music ministry.

*A Handmade Nativity Set that Glows
with Color and Warm Memories*

Crafting a Christmas Crèche

CHARLENE HIEBERT

Christmas is a season rich in memories. It's impossible to celebrate the holidays without calling to mind past Christmases. What memories will you unpack as you take the decorations out of storage this year? What new memories will you pack away for the future when this Christmas is over? Here's a whole-family Christmas project that's sure to produce warm memories—plus a lovely keepsake nativity set—that will last for many years to come.

In the tradition of folk art such as Mexican tin work, these simple metal figures can be cut, tooled, and painted to make a stunning nativity set or brilliantly colored ornaments for your tree. There are eleven figures, and adults and children alike will enjoy creating them.

Tools and Supplies

- Scissors
- Hard lead pencil
- Clear cellophane or masking tape
- Fine-tipped, permanent black marking pen
- Small paint brushes
- Glass paint or enamel paint (available from craft or art stores), or permanent colored markers
- Three aluminum foil cookie sheets, 15 ¼ x 10 ½" (sold in most supermarkets). Choose ones with smooth, plain bottoms, if possible.

Instructions

1. Use a photocopy machine to enlarge the figure patterns (pages 41–42) by 200%. Separate enlarged patterns, cutting approximately ½" outside each figure.

2. Wash the cookie sheets with non-abrasive detergent and a soft cloth or sponge to remove any surface oils. Wearing gloves to protect your hands, cut away the sides of the sheets, leaving only the flat bottom surface.

3. Tape figure patterns onto foil surfaces. Using scissors, cut through the foil around each pattern.

4. Trace over the lines of each pattern with a hard lead pencil. Press firmly to engrave the figures onto the foil, but be careful to avoid tearing the pattern or puncturing the foil. (Children can join in on this step.) Check

reverse side of foil to make sure all lines have been traced. Then remove pattern.

5. Use a fine-tipped black permanent marker to trace over all lines. When ink has dried, cut the figures out with scissors. Stay as close to the outline as possible.

6. Paint the figures, using glass paint, enamel paint, or permanent colored markers. Let everyone get involved in this step. Your creativity and personal

preferences can dictate what colors to use. Make the set uniquely, distinctly your own!

TIPS FOR COLORING THE FIGURES. Young children may find it easier to work with colored markers. Before buying these, test markers on the metal to see how well they color the surface. Enamel paints have more body than glass paint, so they are easier to use. However, glass paints have a beautiful translucence that lets the metal shine through and adds a wonderful glow to the ornaments. You may find it easier to apply glass paint with cotton swabs rather than brushes.

7. When figures are dry, retrace the engraved lines with the black marker. Then fold back the bottom tab along the line at the base of the figure to make a stand for the ornament.

Ideas and Options

- Brass and copper tooling foil is sold at art supply stores and may be substituted for the aluminum. Figures made from these metals look elegant even without paint.

- To make foil Christmas tree ornaments, simply omit the bottom tab on each figure pattern and use a small nail to punch a hole near the top center of the figure. (Do this before painting.) After paint has dried, attach ornament hooks or loop string through the holes.

- You can display your finished nativity pieces in a number of settings. The figures could be arranged on a table or mantel, surrounded by greenery, flowers, and candles or tiny Christmas lights. The glowing colors and the metallic sheen of the figures are accentuated by candles and lights.

IF YOU'RE STILL FEELING CREATIVE after snipping and painting the last nativity figure, you might try making a simple wooden-frame triptych to use as a background for your crèche. The one shown in the above photo was cut from thin pine boards, then stained and hinged together.

For a more elaborate nativity setting, craft your own version of the rustic twig stable shown in the opening photograph. The basic structure is made of twigs gathered from a park or woods. Four forked twigs provide corner supports which anchor the roof beams; straight sticks are used for the roof and the three half-walls with railing. The wall structure and corner supports are pressed and glued into a polystyrene base. The base is covered with flooring strips (available from hobby shops that carry doll house supplies) cut to size and then glued over the polystyrene. ✍

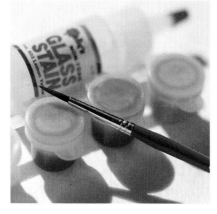

Charlene Hiebert is an editor, writer, and teacher who lives in Elburn, Illinois. She explains: "To me a nativity scene is a small theater. My favorite sets are ones children can touch or have a hand in making. I have seen the true meaning of Christmas take root in children as they work on the figures and then use them to tell and retell the Christmas story."

Photographer Leo Kim spent time in Shanghai, Macao, Hong Kong, and Austria before coming to the United States to study architecture and design. He currently lives and works in Minneapolis, Minnesota where he concentrates on still life photo assignments and black and white portraits.

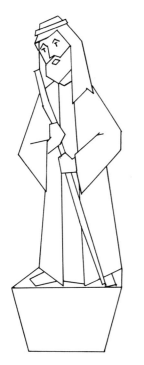

Enlarge patterns 200%

Enlarge patterns 200%

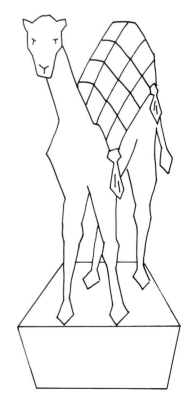

Song for Christmas Eve

MELVA ROREM

Close, close to me I hold the world tonight
Now that the pale white stars are in the sky,
Surrounding earth with the enduring light
Of one great Star that shall not ever die.
Through slender birch, through heavy stands of pine
The singing winds their great, glad secret tell.
The hushed snow, the clouds that intertwine,
Whisper of this most blessed miracle.
The Child is born again! Oh tell it far,
In city streets, in every country road.
Let each one search for stable and for Star;
Let every heart be fit for his abode.
O wondrous Presence, holy, blinding Light—
Close, close to me I hold the world tonight.

From *I Sing of Mary's Child* copyright © 1966 Melva Rorem. Used by permission of Ida Bergeland.

Melva Rorem was a poet, translator, and free-lance writer. For more than twenty years, she was the poetry editor of *Christmas*.

Photographer Joel Sheagren of Minneapolis, Minnesota brings to his work the eye of a commercial photographer and the heart of an avid outdoorsman. The above photograph was taken in Alaska near the Arctic Circle where the temperature was -30˚ F and the snow about six feet deep.

Christmas Closes a Gulf

MOSS HART

I WAS THE CHRISTMAS AFTER my aunt had left the house, and since it was she who always supplied the tree and the presents for my brother and myself, this first Christmas without her was a bleak and empty one.

I remember that I was more or less reconciled to it, because my father had worked only spasmodically throughout the year. Two of our rooms were vacant of boarders and my mother was doing her marketing farther and farther away from our neighborhood. This was always a sign that we were dangerously close to rock bottom, and each time it occurred I came to dread it more. It was one of the vicious landmarks of poverty that I had come to know well and the one I hated most . . .

Obviously Christmas was out of the question—we were barely staying alive. On Christmas Eve my father was very silent during the evening meal. Then he surprised and startled me by turning to me and saying, "Let's take a walk." He had never suggested such a thing before, and moreover, it was a very cold winter's night. I was even more surprised when he said as we left the house, "Let's go down to One Hundred Forty-ninth Street and Westchester Avenue." My heart leaped within me. That was the section where all the big stores were, where at Christmastime open pushcarts full of toys stood packed end-to-end for blocks at a stretch. On other Christmas Eves I had often gone there with my aunt, and from our tour of the carts she had gathered what I wanted the most. My father had known of this, and I joyously concluded that his walk could mean only one thing—he was going to buy me a Christmas present.

On the walk down I was beside myself with delight and an inner relief. It had been a bad year for me, that year of my aunt's going, and I wanted a Christmas present terribly—not a present merely, but a symbol, a token of some sort. I needed some sign from my father or mother that they knew what I was going through and cared for me as much as my aunt and my grandfather did. I am sure they were giving me what mute signs they could, but I did not see them. The idea that my father had managed a Christmas present for me in spite of everything filled me with a sudden peace and lightness of heart I had not known in months.

We hurried on, our heads bent against the wind, to the cluster of lights ahead that was 149th Street and Westchester Avenue, and those lights seemed to me the brightest lights I had ever seen. Tugging at my father's coat, I started down the line of pushcarts. There were all kinds of things I wanted, but since nothing had been said by my father about buying a present, I would merely pause before a pushcart to say, with as much control as I could muster, "Look at that chemistry set!" or, "There's a stamp album!" or, "Look at the printing press!"

Each time my father would pause and ask the pushcart man the price. Then without a word we would move on to the next pushcart. Once or twice he would pick up a toy of some kind and look at it and then at me, as if to suggest this might be something I might like, but I was ten years old and a good deal beyond just a toy; my heart was set on a chemistry set or a printing press. There they were on every pushcart we stopped at, but the price was always the same and soon I looked up and saw we were nearing the end of the line. Only two or three pushcarts remained. My father looked up, too, and I heard him jingle some coins in his pocket. In a flash I knew it all. He'd gotten together about seventy-five cents to buy me a Christmas present, and he hadn't dared to say so in case there was nothing to be had for so small a sum.

As I looked up at him I saw a look of despair and disappointment in his eyes that brought me closer to him than I had ever been in my life. I wanted to throw my arms around him and say, "It doesn't matter. I understand. This is better than a chemistry set or a printing press. I love you."

But instead we stood shivering beside each other for a moment—then turned away from the last two pushcarts and started silently back home. I don't know why the words remained choked up within me. I didn't even take his hand on the way home, nor did he take mine. We were not on that basis. Nor did I ever tell him how close to him I felt that night—that for a little while the concrete wall between father and son had crumbled away and I knew that we were two lonely people struggling to reach each other.

I came close to telling him many years later, but again the moment passed. Again it was Christmas and I was on my way to visit him in Florida. My father was a bright and blooming ninety-one years of age now and I arrived in Florida with my wife to spend Christmas and New Year's with him.

On Christmas Eve we sat in his living room, and while my wife chatted with his nurse and companion, I sat on a sofa across the room with my father, showing him the pictures of his two grandchildren. Suddenly I felt his hand slip into mine. It was the first time in our lives that either of us had ever touched the other. No words were spoken and I went right on turning the pages of the picture album, but my hand remained over his. A few years before I might have withdrawn mine after a moment or two, but now my hand remained; nor did I tell him what I was thinking and feeling. The moment was enough. It had taken forty years for the gulf that separated us to close. ✈

From *Act One* by Moss Hart, © 1959 by Catherine Carlisle Hart and Joseph M. Hyman, Trustees. Used by permission of Random House, Inc.

One of America's most popular and prolific playwrights during the 1930s and 40s, Moss Hart collaborated on such hits as *Face the Music*, *The Man Who Came to Dinner*, and the Pulitzer-Prize-winning *You Can't Take It with You*. Hart died in 1961.

Minneapolis, Minnesota illustrator Bill Cannon writes: "I related particularly well to this story. Alienation happens even in a city full of people. The colorful toys in the illustration embody the warmth and happiness of the holidays in stark contrast to the mood of the father and son."

The Birthplace of God

PHILLIP GUGEL

THE SETTINGS for these nativity scenes by three master painters from the Italian Renaissance include the hayloft of a stable, a ruined shed, and a crumbling shelter. Based on Christian traditions about the Christ child's birthplace, the paintings are rich in allusions to the world into which the holy baby is born.

TINTORETTO

This king-sized oil painting by Jacopo Robusti, better known as Tintoretto—after his father's trade as a dyer—sets the Nativity in a stable's hayloft. An intense orange sky bathes the figures and stable interior with warm light. Above the loft, three gossamer cherubs materialize to peer inside. The play of light and shadow within the stable lends drama as the shepherds offer their adoration and gifts. The basket of eggs and the rooster are gifts which legend says the shepherdesses brought to the child.

While Joseph looks lost in contemplation, Mary welcomes the two women by raising a veil from the holy baby—a symbol of God's revelation of the longed-for Messiah. The Holy Family's placement in a loft above the visitors symbolizes the divine miracle and mystery, as well as the humanity and humility of the Christ child's birth.

Under the loft, a benign ox looks to see what the fuss is all about, a donkey's ghostlike head appears below the shepherds' raised arms, and a rooster pecks at grain. The presence of these creatures underlines the earthiness of the scene. Perched on a pitchfork, a peacock—with its allusions to immortality—reminds the viewer of the child's future death and resurrection.

Tintoretto's complex setting with the robust figures, rich colors, and mysterious warm light, creates an atmosphere which plays upon our senses and boldly announces that God truly has come—among us and for us.

Free-lance art historian Phillip Gugel lives in St. Paul, Minnesota. In addition to speaking and writing about sacred art, he directs the Capitol Hill Refugee Project, a school that teaches English language to adult refugees. This is Gugel's seventeenth consecutive article for *Christmas*.

The Nativity 1577-1581

Scala/Art Resource, NY S0006057. Tintoretto, Jacopo. *The Nativity*. Scuola Grande di S. Rocco, Venice, Italy.

This fifteenth-century Italian Nativity, uses both the cave and a ruined shed as backgrounds for the Christ child's birth. The small hillside cave in Gentile's exquisitely luminous night scene creates an arched frame enfolding the mother and child.

His depiction of the stable as a partially ruined structure has several symbolic allusions. It suggests the decline of the ancient pagan world with the arrival of the holy child. And it alludes to God's promise, recorded in the Old Testament book of Amos, to rebuild King David's fallen tabernacle.

The play of light on figures, objects, spaces, and landscape imparts serenity and visual appeal to Gentile's small composition. Emanating from the infant Jesus, the light creates dramatic interplay with shadows on the shed and the lean-to where the midwives rest. Even the tree supporting the sleeping Joseph is bathed in light and shadow. Gentile was the first Italian painter to portray cast shadows, and his Nativity is the first painting which has its light source within the picture.

The supernatural light which illuminates the cave and shed and casts a soft glow over the kneeling donkey and ox, is complemented by a shimmering night sky. In the upper right portion of the painting, the beams of light from an angel illuminate listening shepherds and the surrounding hillsides. The contours of the remaining hills are defined by the star-filled sky. Gentile was also the first Italian painter to depict night scenes.

This skillful use of rich colors and subtle gradations of light and shadow help to capture the beauty and mystery surrounding Jesus' birth. Though small in its linear dimensions, Gentile's Nativity expands our spiritual dimensions.

The Nativity c. 1423

Scala/Art Resource, NY S0016459. Gentile da Fabriano. *The Nativity*, panel from *The Adoration of the Magi*. Uffizi, Florence, Italy.

Piero's fifteenth-century Nativity is set in a crumbling shelter resembling the kind of hut used by peasants and shepherds at the time of Jesus. The shelter's placement on the edge of a hilltop overlooking both rural and urban landscapes, indicates the sweeping, earth-shattering changes heralded by this child's birth.

Mary's rich blue mantle serves as a frame and a regal cushion for her son, whose arms are raised in supplication. His helplessness and nakedness are further indications of the child's full humanity and humble origins. Mary's kneeling figure expresses adoration of her son, a pose not common in depictions of the virgin until after 1400.

To the left of Jesus' head, the artist has painted a pair of goldfinches, birds fond of thistles and thorns, and symbols of his future passion.

Mary's silent adoration is complemented by the song of strolling minstrels, humanized angels who have been grounded and shorn of wings. Their lutes and viol no longer have strings, the result of damage during restorations to the painting.

Between the celestial musicians and Mary, an ox stands with head lowered in reverent homage, a contrast to the donkey whose raised head and open mouth suggest boisterous braying—an unexpected addition to the angelic chorus.

The presence of a magpie—symbol of misfortune—perched on the roof's edge above the holy family, suggests that the cosmic struggle between this holy child and the forces of Satan has now begun. The final outcome of that struggle is witnessed to by the shepherd's raised hand which points to the star of Bethlehem, an omen of promise beyond the artist's canvas. Perhaps this is what Joseph, seated on a saddle, is contemplating as he attends these unlettered visitors.

Even though sections of the painting are in poor condition, much of its artistry and detail remains. With its marvelous composition and richly symbolic images, Piero's Nativity challenges our imagination and deepens our understanding of the Christmas events.

The Nativity c. 1470
Scala/Art Resource, NY S0083287. Piero della Francesca. *The Nativity*. The National Gallery, London, England.

*When the mayor cancels Jonesboro's nativity display,
Miss Emmaline Effingham Crawford comes to the rescue—
with the help of her entire Sunday school class.*

No Room for Jesus
in Jonesboro

ELIZABETH RICE HANDFORD

EMMALINE SLAPPED HER WHITE WICKER BREAKFAST TRAY onto her bed with more vigor than she intended. Her cup of herbal tea sloshed onto her wheat toast. "If I've got to retire," she said, hitching up her gown and climbing back into bed, "I might as well try to enjoy it."

For forty-five years Emmaline had worked at the post office. Last month the postmaster had told her she had to retire. "I'm sorry, Miss Emmaline, but it's the law."

"Law or no law," she said, dipping her soggy toast into her soft-boiled egg, "a body needs to be needed."

She unrolled the morning newspaper and stared at the headline. "There, now! Just look at that!"

Her trembling finger traced the words:

MAYOR CANCELS PARK NATIVITY SCENE

Jonesboro Mayor Frederick Parker today instructed park employees not to set up the traditional nativity scene in Central Park this year. The crèche has been a part of the city's yearly Christmas decorations for more than thirty years. Had civil liberties groups protested the religious figures displayed on public property? Mayor Parker answered, "No, but as mayor, I have an obligation to protect the religious liberties of all."

Emmaline permitted herself a feminine snort. The same old Freddie Parker. Acting just like he did when he was a kid in knickers and the terror of East Ninth Street. He doesn't care a hoot about religious liberty. He's running for re-election.

Emmaline moved restlessly to the bathroom. Somehow the loss of the familiar Christmas crèche in the park was just too much. "I wish somebody would put Freddie Parker in his place," she said to her reflection in the mirror, "and put Jesus back where he belongs!"

"Well, Emmaline," her reflection asked, "why don't you do something about it?"

Emmaline glared back. "You know there's not a blessed thing I can do. I'm too old now even to sort mail."

The reflected Emmaline raised an eyebrow. "So the children of Jonesboro will just have to grow up without knowing about Jesus at Christmas?"

Aggrieved, Emmaline put down her unused toothbrush. "What do you suggest I do about it?"

"Go see the mayor."

"You remember what a rotten kid Mayor Frederick Parker was when he lived next door to us. He'd sneer at me."

"A sneer never killed anybody."

"I might lose my postal pension. And if I starve, you starve."

"Emmaline Effingham Crawford: you know very well you won't lose your pension for being brave enough to stand up to the mayor."

"I know," Emmaline answered herself brokenly, "I need to be brave." She jerked away from the mirror's reflection, stabbed to the heart with memory.

Nineteen forty-two. The Jonesboro train depot. She and her Johnny on the train platform for their last precious moments together before he joined his army unit overseas. "Be brave for my sake, Mrs. Johnny Crawford," he'd said with a kiss.

So she'd been brave for the sake of her young and brave husband.

Three months later, a yellow telegram arrived from the war office. Johnny had died in a fair French meadow when he stepped on a land mine.

Then they told her to be brave for the sake of her unborn child. So she'd been brave when that tiny scrap of unfinished humanity, already fatherless, blundered its way into an unready world. Two days later she'd buried the child Johnny had never seen.

So there was no reason for Emmaline ever to be brave again. Except that God was God, and that was enough. For forty-five years Emmaline Effingham Crawford worked at the post office and taught her Sunday school class, living with a bravery she would have called stubbornness if she'd thought of it at all.

She turned back to the mirror. "All right, Emmaline: we'll try it."

She brushed her teeth and dressed quickly, then hurried to catch the bus that went to city hall. There, in those surroundings, she found it hard to think of the mayor as little Freddie Parker, the neighborhood bane. His secretary politely explained that the mayor was in conference and very busy. Could her business wait until January?

"January? Oh, no. I need to ask him to let them put up the Christmas crèche in the park."

"I'm sorry, Mrs. Crawford. The mayor's mind is quite made up about the Christmas scene."

That afternoon, to Emmaline's surprise, the mayor phoned. "Of course I remember you, Miss Emmaline. I'm sorry I was busy when you stopped by."

"Freddie—Mr. Mayor—please let them put the Christmas crèche up. You can't have a Christmas without Christ."

The mayor's voice colored with a hint of a sneer. "Miss Emmaline, there is no room for displays of Jesus on public property in Jonesboro."

After he hung up, his words echoed in Emmaline's mind: "No room for Jesus in Jonesboro."

On Sunday morning, those words were still on her mind when she gathered her Sunday school class of eight- and nine-year-olds around her. "There was no room for Jesus in the inn at Bethlehem," she said sadly. "And now, in our very own town, there is no room for Jesus. What shall we do about it?"

All of the children collectively knitted their brows to indicate that they were thinking very seriously.

"Let's sue the mayor," Eddie said.

Emmaline spent a lot of time talking to the Lord about Eddie. He mimicked his elders' platitudes while plotting outrageous escapades. He was a lot like Simon Peter, she decided. If the Lord could use Peter, couldn't he find some good use for Eddie Snyder?

Emmaline hugged him. "That's an idea. Keep thinking."

"The parade," Brandy said softly, unexpectedly. "We could be in the Christmas parade."

Emmaline had never gotten over the shock of the name Brandy's mother had given this elfin, moody child. "A parade, Brandy?"

"The Christmas parade is next Sunday afternoon. We could have a float with the manger scene on it."

"Neat-o!" the children chorused.

"I get dibs on being a wise man," said Charlie.

"I'll be King Herod with the sword," said Eddie.

Anastasia said softly, "I'll be an angel."

"Angels aren't black," Alice protested.

Again Brandy surprised Emmaline. "Yes, they are," she said. "Red and yellow, black and white, they are precious in His sight—that's what the Bible says."

Emmaline hid a smile. "I think Anastasia will make a lovely angel. But children, let's not get carried away. Where will we get a float? A truck to pull it? Costumes? Can we get ready in a week?"

The children airily dismissed such questions. Each child knew someone who might help.

"All right, if the pastor says it's all right, we'll try it."

Unfortunately, the pastor thought it was a great idea, so Emmaline was committed in spite of herself.

On Monday she phoned city hall to get information about the parade. She was horrfied to learn that a registration fee of fifty dollars was required.

Anxiously she dialed the church. "Pastor, I didn't know there was a registration fee, and . . ."

The pastor interrupted gently. "How much do you need?"

"Fifty dollars," she said miserably. "I can pay it back. Twenty-five dollars when my check comes, and the rest next month."

"Nonsense, Emmaline. The church can handle that."

Wednesday, Brandy's mother phoned. "Are you actually intending to let those little children stand for two hours on an open float in the middle of winter without coats?"

"If you'd rather Brandy didn't . . ."

"No, no. She's set her heart on being Mary. I'm just warning you that I hold you personally accountable. And please talk her out of using that stupid doll for the baby Jesus. Half of its hair is gone, and one eye is knocked out."

And, Emmaline thought wryly, as Eddie pointed out, it's a girl doll, too. Aloud, she said, "It meant so much to Brandy. I think we can keep it wrapped up so no one will notice."

"We'd all better pray it doesn't snow Sunday," said Brandy's mother as she hung up.

It did not snow on Sunday, but there was a cold, penetrating mist which threatened to turn to rain. Their float was ready, if amateurish. Fred Sims, whose pickup truck they were using to pull the float, carefully drove up to the appointed staging place.

The parade marshal was sweating profusely in spite of the cold. He consulted his clipboard. "Sixth Street Community Church? You follow Number 22—the horses."

Emmaline stared at the marshal, her faded eyes filled with dismay. The children had tacked a skirt of white nylon on their float. It sagged down to the pavement in places. If they had to follow the horses . . . ! Emmaline swallowed. "Follow the horses?"

"Right! Behind Entry 22, Sam's Feed and Seed."

She turned restlessly to check the children. They stood on the float in stiff-kneed array, a dismal caricature of a Christmas nativity scene. Their eyes were fastened on her. Her anxiety had seeped into them. She straightened the hand-lettered sign. It looked crude and, in this place, abrasive: "IS THERE NO ROOM FOR JESUS IN JONESBORO EITHER?"

"But the horses . . . " she began again.

The marshal couldn't bear the distressed look in the old lady's face. "You don't like following the horses, lady? OK, you go in front of the horses, behind the baby motorcycle team."

Emmaline's smile illuminated her face. "Thank you. We don't mean to be a bother."

She hurried back to the truck, climbed into the passenger side. "Pull in behind those motorcycles, Fred." She poked her head out the window and called back, "Hold on tight, children; we're going to move."

Fred's hay rack made a nice manger scene, Emmaline decided, watching through the back window. Little Brandy sat on a bale of hay, already posed, leaning over the manger where her battered doll nestled in the hay. Benjamin, dressed in his father's bathrobe, stood behind her, an earnest and youthful Joseph. Eddie had been persuaded to exchange his King Herod sword for a wise man's cookie tin gilded to look like a gift of gold. Anastasia glowed in angel gauze, her brown face cherubic, her hand already lifted to the crowds like a beauty queen in the Parade of Roses.

Eventually the unwieldy parade began to move, undulating like an uncoordinated centipede through the throngs of people lining Main Street.

"Just think, Miss Emmaline," Fred said cheerfully, "the governor is on the reviewing stand with the mayor. You are going to be real proud today!"

Just then the precision motorcycle squad

slowed down to execute an intricate set of moving figure eights. Fred was forced to ease to a stop.

A terrified screech cut through the noise. Emmaline threw open the door, tore back to the float, and found Brandy and Benjamin both hysterical. The horses pulling Sam's Feed and Seed float had thrust their big heads around the two terrified children to snatch greedily from the manger every tuft of hay they could reach. Brandy, thinking they would eat her doll, beat against them with impotent fists.

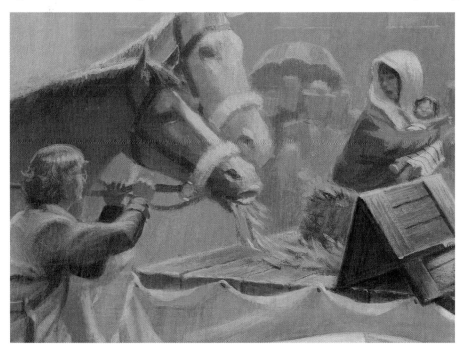

"Sir! Sir!" Emmaline yelled. "Look what your horses are doing!"

Sam—or whoever it was driving Sam's Feed and Seed entry—shrugged helplessly. "I can't stop 'em, ma'am, when they're so close. Tell your driver to pull ahead."

"Can't do it, Miss Emmaline," Fred called out. "I'd run over the midget motorcyclists." He climbed stiffly out of the truck and walked back. "Here now, stop that!" he said gruffly, pulling back on the horses' bridles. The horses pulled and tugged, reluctant to leave their free meal. Spectators clapped, and he bowed.

"Hey, mister, the parade's going off without you," someone yelled.

"Jump in, Miss Emmaline."

"I can't leave the children, Fred. You drive, and I'll walk beside them."

And that's exactly what Emmaline did for the next interminable mile.

Sometimes she pushed with all her might against the great strength of the hungry horses behind her. Sometimes, when Fred was able to get ahead of them, she encircled a sobbing Brandy, and whispered encouragement to Benjamin, held upright only by his paralyzed terror. The mist turned to rain. The cardboard props began to droop. Angel wings sagged. Brandy clutched her battered doll, its arms and legs flailing, its matted hair awry, its one eye staring reproachfully. Emmaline's eyes began to water from the cold, and her nose started to drip. Holding the children as she did, she could not walk upright, and the awkward angle threw every stiffened and arthritic joint out of place.

"Fred," she hissed. "Let's get out of here! Turn off at the next corner."

But every cross street was blocked by spectators. "Miss Emmaline, you drive. I'll walk."

Emmaline shook her head miserably. "I can't drive a stick shift, Fred."

When they reached the reviewing stand, the horses were still rooting around the bare manger. The sign hung tiredly, crookedly, sagging at the edges. Tears fell down Emmaline's wrinkled cheeks, in spite of her efforts to wipe them away. She looked up to see Mayor Frederick Parker pointing derisively at the float, laughing with the governor. At that terrible moment, the flash of a news photographer's camera caught them, capturing every dreadful detail with merciless accuracy.

The next morning, Emmaline lay in her bed and looked at that picture. They'd printed it in full color, five columns wide, on the front page of the Monday paper. Emmaline looked dispassionately at her own ravaged, wrinkled face; saw Brandy's doll, tattered and naked; the pointed finger and sneer of the mayor; dear Anastasia's dimpled grin and brown hand raised in papal benediction; the horses caught with teeth bared, lunging for the last wisp of hay. But, thank God,

the crooked sign was still readable: "IS THERE NO ROOM FOR JESUS IN JONESBORO EITHER?"

Lying in bed sipping hot lemon juice and honey for her terrible cold, Emmaline felt her humiliation unendurable. She'd embarrassed the church family, let down her Sunday school children, given cause for rejoicing to the Enemy—and especially Freddie Parker. All she could hope for, she decided, was that this cold would turn into a case of terminal pneumonia.

The phone rang. The pastor's voice sang with excitement. "Seen the paper, Miss Emmaline?"

Emmaline groaned. "I know. I know. You want my resignation."

"Oh, you dear, foolish woman! Don't you know the whole town is talking about Jesus today? Isn't that exactly what we wanted? The wire services have picked up that picture, and tomorrow people all over the country will be asking themselves if they have room for Jesus!"

Her next phone call was from Eddie.

"Eddie? Are you sick?"

"Nope, I'm in school," he answered happily, "only the teacher got tired of my sniffling and sent me to the health room."

Emmaline winced. She deserved to be sick, but not the poor children. "Eddie, do you have permission to be using the phone there?"

Eddie ignored her question. "Miss Emmaline, we're famous!"

"Infamous, you mean," was Emmaline's tired reply.

Her sarcasm was wasted on Eddie. "The guys at school saw us on TV last night. They think our Sunday school class is neat. They all want to come next Sunday."

"That's great, Eddie. Now hang up."

Emmaline thought she couldn't bear another phone call. She took the phone off the hook and burrowed her head under the quilt.

She wept, then dozed, and was awakened by the doorbell. Groggily she reached for a robe and staggered to the door.

Brandy's mother stood there, waving the newspaper picture.

Emmaline's heart skipped a beat. "Brandy! Is she sick, too?"

Cynthia Walker shook her head. "No, Brandy's fine," she said. "But I'm not."

"Oh, my dear, what's wrong?"

"I saw this beautiful picture and realized how much my little girl loves Jesus, and how proud she was to stand up for him in that parade."

Emmaline thought she must be hallucinating. Maybe she had a fever. But no, Brandy's mother was really standing there, her mascara smudged, pride shattered, desperation in her eyes.

"I'm so ashamed of all the mean things I said about the parade and Brandy's stupid doll," she said, "and I'm so tired of being the kind of person I am." Now the words were pouring out, along with tears that left dark tracks of mascara down her cheeks. "Oh, Mrs. Crawford," she sobbed, "I haul Brandy off to Sunday school, and I pick her up. But I never set foot inside church. I haven't given God the time of day! And I feel just rotten."

Emmaline's heart sang. Bless Freddie Parker's devious heart! In spite of himself, Freddie had accomplished God's business! And bless that unquenchable conscience of yours, Emmaline Effingham Crawford, that wouldn't stop nagging you!

"Please," Brandy's mother was saying, "do you have the time to help me? I want to make room in my heart for Jesus."

"Oh, my dear," Emmaline said, opening wide the door, "of course I have time. Please, please, do come in!" ❧

Originally published in *The Joyful Woman*, Chattanooga, Tennessee, 1988.

Elizabeth Rice Handford of Greenville, South Carolina, writes: "I long for people in this generation—especially my grandchildren—to experience the truth that God became a baby to redeem this fallen world. A chance complaint that a float in the local Christmas parade was nearly ruined when horses ate hay from the crèche, gave me a vehicle to tell the story afresh."

Steve Johnson and Lou Fancher of Minneapolis, Minnesota have worked as a collaborative team for ten years. Together they have illustrated seven children's books. They are currently working on their eighth book, a children's story by Dr. Seuss.

A Stable Lamp Is Lighted

Richard Wilbur

A stable lamp is lighted
Whose glow shall wake the sky;
The stars shall bend their voices,
And ev'ry stone shall cry.
And ev'ry stone shall cry,
And straw like gold shall shine;
A barn shall harbor heaven,
A stall become a shrine.

*T*his child through David's city
Shall ride in triumph by;
The palm shall strew its branches,
And ev'ry stone shall cry.
And ev'ry stone shall cry,
Though heavy, dull, and dumb,
And lie within the roadway
To pave his kingdom come.

Yet he shall be forsaken
And yielded up to die;
The sky shall groan and darken,
And ev'ry stone shall cry.
And ev'ry stone shall cry
For stony hearts of men:
God's blood upon the spearhead,
God's love refused again.

But now, as at the ending,
The low is lifted high;
The stars shall bend their voices,
And ev'ry stone shall cry.
And ev'ry stone shall cry
In praises of the child
By whose descent among us
The worlds are reconciled.

Here's a festive holiday menu featuring memorable foods and memory-making fun!

MERRY MEMORIES
A Christmas Brunch

SANDRA BURROWES AND PAMELA JOHNSON

Wake up to holiday smells of ginger, cinnamon, and cloves. Here's a memory-making brunch to delight the imagination—and the tummy!

We asked friends and family for their best "we-always-make-it-at-Christmas" recipes and then combined them into a fabulous brunch menu. Don't be surprised if gingerbread pancakes, overnight French toast, or the very special English Christmas cake become holiday traditions at your house!

Menu
Gingerbread Pancakes

Overnight French Toast

Bacon, Sausage

Twelve-Fruit Compote

English Christmas Cake

Sparkling Fruit Spritzer, Milk, Coffee

Memory Makers

* Gather the family to help make the Christmas cake batter. Everyone gets three big stirs and three secret wishes.
* Let children use cookie cutters to turn gingerbread pancakes into favorite holiday shapes.
* Set your table with heirloom dishes and linens.
* Decorate the table with favorite family photos, keepsake ornaments, or homemade gifts.
* Before or after brunch, read aloud the biblical Christmas story from pages 6-9 in this book. Assign the angels' lines to be read by children. Then sing one or two favorite carols.

Colorful foods, keepsake ornaments, and family photos lend a festive flair to your holiday table.

GINGERBREAD PANCAKES

Makes 12 large "gingerbread boy" pancakes

3 cups flour
6 tsp baking powder
3 tsp cocoa
1 ½ tsp powdered ginger
¾ tsp ground cinnamon
¾ tsp ground cloves
6 Tbs ground hazelnuts (optional)
3 cups milk
6 egg whites
6 Tbs dark molasses
6 tsp vegetable oil for greasing pan

large gingerbread boy cookie cutter (or Christmas cookie cutters)

Sift flour, baking powder, cocoa, ginger, cinnamon and cloves into large bowl. Stir in hazelnuts (if using).

In medium bowl, whisk together milk, egg whites, and molasses. Make a well in flour mixture and pour milk mixture into it. Stir just enough to moisten. Batter will be lumpy.

Brush a large, non-stick frying pan with a little oil. Place over medium heat until hot. Ladle in batter, forming a rectangle approximately the size of cookie cutter. Cook for two minutes, then flip and cook for two more minutes.

Press cookie cutter into the pancake. Discard trimmed pieces. Transfer gingerbread boys to ovenproof platter and keep in warm 200° oven until ready to serve. Serve with syrup, sweetened whipped cream, or a warmed fruit compote.

OVERNIGHT FRENCH TOAST

Makes 12 pieces

¼ cup butter, room temperature (½ stick)
12 slices of French bread, ¾" thick
6 eggs
1 ½ cups milk
¼ cup sugar
2 Tbs light corn syrup or maple syrup
1 tsp vanilla
½ tsp salt

Spread butter over bottom of large, heavy baking pan with 1"-high sides. Arrange bread slices in pan in a single layer. Beat eggs, milk, sugar, syrup, vanilla, and salt to blend, then pour over the bread. Turn bread to coat evenly. Cover with plastic wrap and refrigerate overnight.

Preheat oven to 400°F. Remove plastic wrap and bake for 10 minutes. Turn bread and continue baking until just golden, about 4 minutes longer. Transfer cooked toast to ovenproof plate and keep in warm 200° oven until ready to serve. Serve with warmed maple syrup or raspberry jam.

TWELVE-FRUIT COMPOTE

About 12 servings

3 cups water
1 lb mixed dried fruits—pears, figs, apricots, peaches
1 cup pitted prunes
½ cup raisins or currants
1 cup pitted, canned sweet cherries and their juice
2 apples, peeled and sliced
½ cup fresh or frozen cranberries
¼ cup sugar
1 lemon, thinly sliced
6 whole cloves
2 cinnamon sticks
1 orange—grated, peeled, and sectioned
½ cup fresh seedless grapes
½ cup pomegranate seeds
½ cup fruit-flavored brandy or apple juice

Combine water, dried fruits, prunes, and raisins in a 6-quart kettle. Bring to boil, then cover and simmer about 10 minutes, until fruit is plump and tender.

Add cherries, apples, and cranberries. Stir in sugar, lemon, and spices. Cover and simmer 5 minutes longer. Remove from heat.

Grate orange peel and set aside. Peel and section orange, removing skin and white membrane. Add to fruits in kettle.

Stir in grapes and brandy or apple juice. Stir in grated orange peel. Cover and let stand 15 minutes. Remove cinnamon sticks, whole cloves, and lemon. Sprinkle pomegranate seeds over compote and serve in decorative bowl.

SPARKLING FRUIT SPRITZER

Makes 12 glasses

2 cans (6 oz) frozen lemonade concentrate, thawed
1 cup cold water
14 oz chilled ginger ale
14 oz chilled sparkling water
1 bottle (25 oz) chilled white sparkling catawba grape juice

Combine all ingredients in large 3-quart pitcher. Serve immediately.

ENGLISH CHRISTMAS CAKE

This recipe is part of a generations-old family tradition. The delicious array of dried fruits and nuts baked into this cake represent the bounty of the fall harvest. The cake is made the day after Thanksgiving and stored, well-wrapped, in the refrigerator until the week before Christmas. Then the almond paste is applied and the cake frosted and put on display until Christmas Day, when the family eagerly takes part in a ceremonial tasting.

1 cup butter or margarine (2 sticks)
1 cup sugar
5 eggs, separated
1 cup raisins
1 cup currants
1 cup golden raisins (if not available, double amount of raisins)
½ cup chopped almonds
4 oz chopped mixed fruit peel
4 oz glacé cherries
grated rind of 2 lemons
1 cup flour
½ tsp baking powder
1 tsp ground ginger
1 tsp cinnamon
½ tsp allspice (optional)

THE DAY AFTER THANKSGIVING
Cream butter or margarine and sugar together until light and fluffy. Beat in egg yolks, one at a time. In another bowl, whisk egg whites until stiff and gently fold into creamed mixture.

In a separate bowl, mix together raisins, currants, almonds, cherries, peel, and lemon rind.

In a large bowl, sift together flour, baking powder, ginger, cinnamon, and allspice. Alternately fold fruit and sifted flour into the butter-egg mixture. *

Turn batter into a Springform pan that has been greased and then lined with waxed paper. Smooth the top of batter, leaving a small indentation in center so that when cake rises, it creates a level surface.

Bake on the middle shelf of a 300°F oven for two hours, until firm. A toothpick inserted into the center should come out clean. Cool in the pan for one hour. Then carefully remove from pan, leaving waxed paper around cake. Place on a wire rack. When thoroughly cooled, cover cake first in plastic wrap, then in aluminum foil. Slip wrapped cake into a food storage bag, seal, and store in refrigerator.

An important tradition involves all family members in mixing the cake. Each person takes three big stirs and makes three wishes (with eyes closed!)—

a clever and painless way to get a heavy batter mixed.

THE WEEK BEFORE CHRISTMAS
Remove cake from wrappings and add almond paste, icing, and decorations.

ALMOND PASTE

2 7-oz tubes of almond paste (found in the baking section of many grocery stores)
any jam, slightly warmed

Brush top and sides of cake with slightly warmed jam. This helps adhere the almond paste to the cake. Roll almond paste on a powdered-sugar-coated board to ¼" thickness. Using the base of Springform pan as a guide, cut a circle of almond paste to cover cake top. Transfer circle to cake. From remaining paste, cut strips to cover cake sides. Pinch the paste where top and sides meet, creating a smooth edge. Leave uncovered at room temperature for 24 hours to set.

ROYAL ICING

1 ½ lbs confectioners' sugar
3 egg whites
lemon juice
2 Tbs Crisco or other solid white shortening

Sift confectioners' sugar into bowl. Make hollow in center and add egg whites, beating well with a wooden spoon. Very gradually, stir in lemon juice until icing is thick, smooth, and very white. Ice the cake, covering top and sides. After icing has set (about 2–3 hours), decorate the cake with cloth ribbon, or add tiny figurines to form a Christmas tableau on top of the cake. (Press figurines into icing while it is still soft.) ❦

Pamela Johnson is Director of Product Management on the Augsburg Fortress book team. She has designed and catered events for as few as two, and as many as two hundred people, and she regularly prepares summer "porch parties" for friends and family at her home in Minneapolis. Her recipe for twelve-fruit compote is a Christmas morning tradition at her house.

Sandra Burrowes is Product Line Manager for the Augsburg Fortress book team. She enjoys gathering family and friends for dinner parties at her home in Eagan, Minnesota. As a result, a favorite pasttime has become the creation of special cakes and formal desserts. The recipe for English Christmas cake comes from her husband's family, where it has been handed down for generations.

Photography by Leo Kim, Minneapolis, MN.

Christmas Memories

How We Spent Christmas Eve

_____

Christmas Day Highlights

_____

Favorite Gifts

_____

A Special Memory

_____

Our Holiday Guests   Their Greetings and Wishes

_____   _____

_____   _____

_____   _____

_____   _____

_____   _____

_____   _____

_____   _____

_____   _____

(Attach a Christmas photo here.)

Dan Reed is an illustrator and painter who lives in Providence, Rhode Island. The techniques he uses are based on pre-Renaissance panel-painting common in Italy in the thirteenth to fourteenth centuries.